Peterson First Guide to the SOLAR SYSTEM

Jay M. Pasachoff

Planet-finding Maps by
Wil Tirion

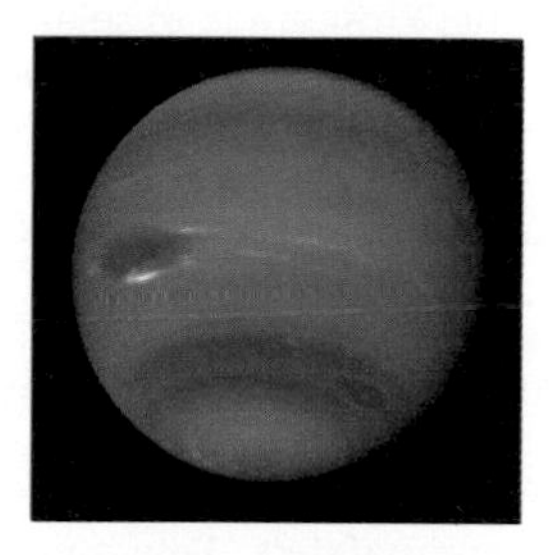

HOUGHTON
MIFFLIN
COMPANY
•
BOSTON
1990

Library of Congress Cataloging-in-Publication Data

Pasachoff, Jay M.
Peterson first guide to the solar system.

Running title: First guide to solar systems.
Summary: A basic field guide for beginning
observers of the solar system, introducing
information on the locations and characteristics of
the planets, sun, comets, meteors, and other objects
in our solar system.
1. Astronomy — Juvenile literature. 2. Solar
system — Juvenile literature. 3. Astronomy —
Amateur's manuals.
[1. Astronomy. 2. Solar system. 3. Astronomy
— Observers' manuals] I. Peterson, Roger Tory,
(date) II. Tirion, Wil. III. Title. IV. Title: First
guide to solar systems.
QB46.P377 1990 520 89–24744
ISBN 0-395-52451-2

Printed in Italy

NIL 10 9 8 7 6 5 4 3 2 1

Editor's Note

The skies belong to everyone. The moon, the planets, and the sun are available to us every day, whenever it is clear. They are our nearest neighbors in the universe. Thus it is fitting that they receive special attention in their own *First Guide.*

Everyone enjoys looking at the sky, much as live birds are always a pleasure to look at. And in both cases, knowing what you are looking at helps you enjoy looking more. My *Field Guide to the Birds* has been designed to help novices be able to identify birds in the field, without having to learn technical points. My *First Guide to the Birds* helps beginners get started with the most common birds.

In the same way, Jay M. Pasachoff's second edition of *A Field Guide to the Stars and Planets* is both up-to-date and thorough, yet easy to use. His *First Guide to Astronomy* provided an attractive introduction to the universe. Now, in this new *First Guide,* he has singled out the objects that are closest to us the moon, the planets, the sun, comets, asteroids, and meteors — and given them the special attention they deserve. He has provided us with a handy little guide that mixes information on observing our neighboring planets and their moons from Earth with the latest beautiful images taken from the ground and from space.

I hope you will take this book with you when you next step outside at night. It will help you identify the features that make a face on the moon, and will help you find and identify planets in the sky. And it will tell you the answers to many questions about what these objects are like.

This *First Guide to the Solar System* and its companion *First Guide to Astronomy* are designed for anyone who is curious about the night sky. When you are ready to look further, we hope you will take up the full-fledged *Field Guide to the Stars and Planets.*

Roger Tory Peterson

Introducing the Solar System

The sun, nine planets and their dozens of moons, and other objects like comets and asteroids make up our solar system — our neighborhood in the universe. Light can travel from the sun — the only star in our neighborhood — to us on Earth in only eight minutes. It takes light over four years to travel from the sun to the next closest star, which is much farther away. Though we can learn a lot about the stars by studying light and other signals (such as radio waves) they give off, it is only objects in our solar system that are close enough that we can have any hope of visiting them.

The major objects in the solar system are the sun and nine planets: Mercury, Venus, Earth, Mars, Jupiter, Saturn, Uranus, Neptune, and Pluto. You can remember them, in order of

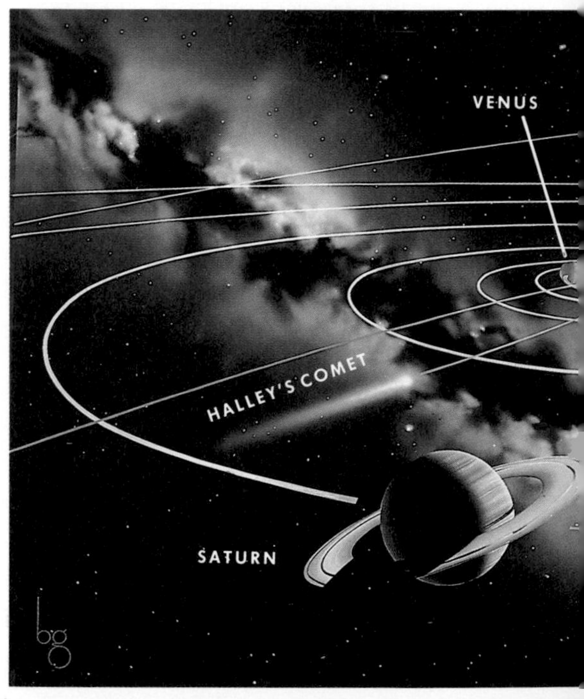

their distance from the sun, as having the same first letters as the words in the phrase, "My Very Educated Mother Just Sent Us Nine Pizzas."

As you see in the picture below, the inner four planets — Mercury, Venus, Earth, and Mars — are fairly small. Mercury and Venus have no moons, the Earth has one moon, and Mars has two tiny moons. The next four planets are giants. Each has many moons. Each of these four planets — not just Saturn — also has rings. The outermost planet — Pluto — is small and ringless, with only one small moon.

In recent years, spacecraft from Earth have made close-up visits to all the planets except Pluto. On the pages that follow, we show a variety of pictures of the planets, taken with cameras and telescopes on Earth and in space.

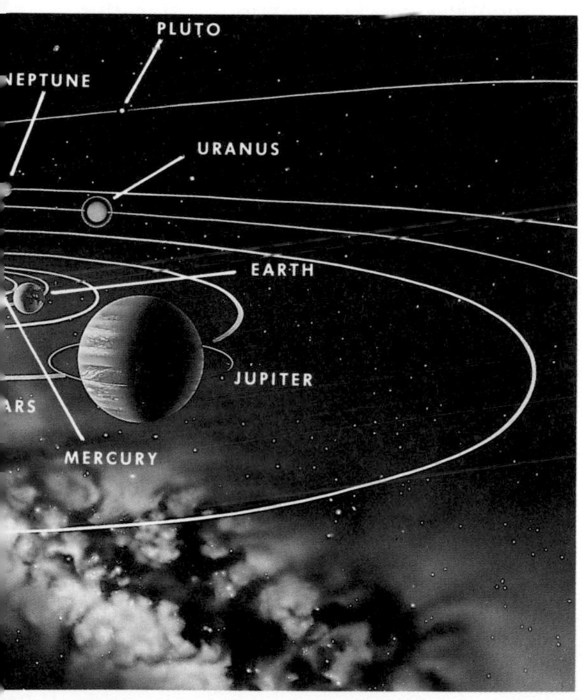

In the picture below, we see the planets displayed from left to right in order of their distance from the sun. The sizes of the four innermost planets — Mercury, Venus, Earth (bluish), and Mars (reddish) — are shown to scale in comparison with the outer planets and the sun, at bottom.

Jupiter and Saturn are quite spectacular next to our puny world. Even Jupiter's Great Red Spot, a giant storm that has been observed for hundreds of years, is much larger than our Earth. Jupiter's horizontal bands are clouds in its atmosphere, which is very thick. Saturn's bands of clouds show less clearly because Saturn is farther from the sun and therefore colder. Uranus and Neptune appear bluish or greenish because methane gas in their thick atmospheres absorbs all the other colors in sunlight (which contains all colors) except bluish green. No detail can be seen on tiny Pluto from Earth.

Our solar system contains a wide variety of astronomical objects. The sun is a star, the closest one to us. Like all stars, the sun shines

with energy it makes in its interior. Planets and their moons shine with reflected sunlight. So do asteroids and meteoroids.

Finding the Planets in the Sky

The planets orbit the sun more or less in the same plane, called the *ecliptic*. As a result, the planets go across the night sky within the same band above our horizon. Mercury and Venus are never far from the sun in the sky. Maps in this book (see pp. 52–55, 66–67, and 78–79) show where Mars, Jupiter, and Saturn can be seen within the band of sky.

There is another way you can pick out the planets from the background of stars in the night sky: unlike stars, planets don't twinkle. The Earth's atmosphere makes the stars dance about and change slightly in brightness from moment to moment. The stars are distant twinkling points of light to us, while the planets are so close that we see them as tiny, steadily gleaming disks. The sunlight reflected from different parts of the planets' disks averages out, making the planets gleam steadily.

The Earth

The Earth is interesting both in its own right — as our home in the solar system — and also as an example of a solar-system member. The kinds of features we find on Earth are often examples of what we can find on other planets. For example, mountain ranges are typical not only of the Earth but also of Mercury, Venus, Mars, our moon, and the moons of other planets.

Only when astronauts traveled into space and looked back at the Earth did we realize how fragile a planet we live on. Photographs like the one below, taken by astronauts en route to the moon, showed us that we are on an oasis in space. We must learn to keep our planet safe and habitable.

The Earth, photographed from the Apollo 16 spacecraft en route to the moon. Most of the Earth was covered with clouds, but much of the United States and Mexico are visible.

Once outside the Earth's atmosphere, spacecraft could study the Earth in new ways. The photograph below was taken with ultraviolet light — light much shorter in wavelength than visible light. Since we can't see ultraviolet light, the original black-and-white photograph was color-coded to show different brightnesses of ultraviolet coming from hydrogen gas. In red, we see the *geocorona* — the faint halo of low-density hydrogen gas that surrounds the Earth. At lower right, the reddish-colored extension of the Earth's edge actually comes from an aurora — the "southern lights" — near the Earth's South Pole. (In the Northern Hemisphere, we see the "northern lights," an aurora that sometimes forms near the Earth's North Pole.) The black sky seen by the astronauts is shown here in blue.

In this view from the moon, the Earth appears as a crescent. Since half the Earth is always lighted by the sun, the sun must be off to the left, and farther away than the Earth from the camera. We are used to seeing the moon, not the Earth, as a crescent (see p. 20). Traveling in space often gives us new perspectives on familiar objects.

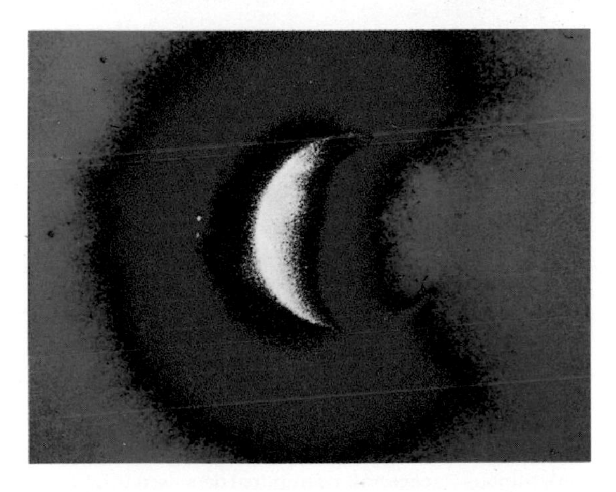

This photograph taken by Apollo 16 astronauts on the moon shows the Earth's geocorona, a halo of faint hydrogen light. The astronauts couldn't see it — it shows only in pictures taken with ultraviolet light. This photograph uses false colors to show brightness.

Earth

Space-shuttle astronauts are about 185 miles (300 km) above the Earth's surface. The views they get of the Earth are spectacular. At that altitude, spacecraft or satellites orbit the Earth in about 90 minutes, so the astronauts see 18 sunrises and 18 sunsets each day.

The higher a satellite is above the Earth, the longer it takes to orbit. At an altitude of 22,000 miles (35,000 km) above the Earth's surface, a satellite takes 24 hours to orbit the Earth. The Earth rotates at the same rate underneath, so to a person on Earth, the satellite appears to be hovering overhead. We therefore put communications satellites in

The National Oceanographic and Atmospheric Administration's Nimbus 7 spacecraft transmitted data used to make this false-color view showing the temperature of the Atlantic Ocean off the eastern United States. The satellite's infrared scanners, which are sensitive to differences in temperature, picked up the warm waters of the Gulf Stream as it meanders toward northern Europe.

"geosynchronous orbits" — synchronized with Earth's. Many of our television pictures are relayed to us by these satellites. Weather satellites are also in geosynchronous orbits. They photograph the Earth every few minutes and send their information down to Earth by radio.

NASA is planning a "Mission to Planet Earth," using space satellites to monitor the health of our planet. Satellites can monitor the ozone in our air, the fish in our oceans, the temperature of the oceans and the continents, smoke from forest fires, eruptions of volcanoes, and many other aspects of Earth and of life on it.

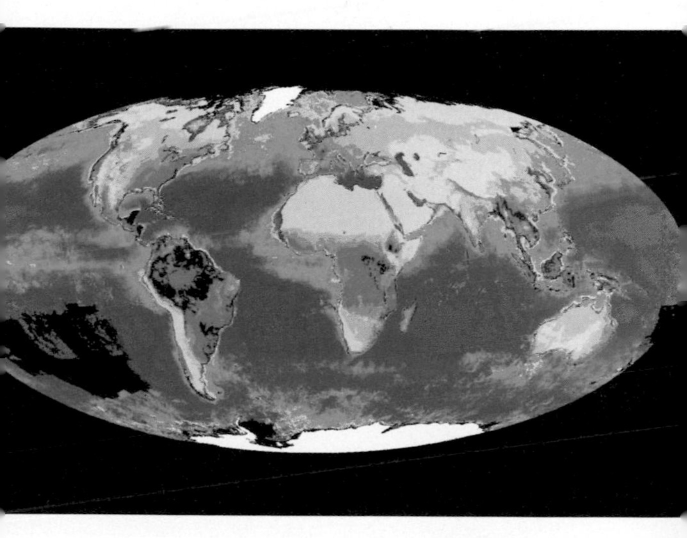

Satellite data have been combined to show the Earth's vegetation. Red and orange in the ocean (especially near the coasts) show where floating plankton, in this case microscopic plants, are most concentrated. Note that the plankton make the equator show up well in the Pacific Ocean. Chlorophyll and leaves show as green on land.

Earth

Photographs from space give us a global perspective. The curvature of the Earth is clearly visible in the photo below. Note also the thin, fragile nature of the Earth's atmosphere, and how quickly the blackness of space begins.

This view from the space shuttle shows Florida in the foreground, and extends northward over more of the United States. The urban area around Miami is at lower right. The Cape Canaveral area, from which the shuttles are launched, extends into the Atlantic Ocean on Florida's east coast.

Studies of the Earth's weather from da
day have provided valuable information t
has more than paid back the cost of the sp
program. We learn even more about basics o
weather and climate by studying the Earth from space. The photograph below shows the circular pattern a storm has. Large tropical storms like these are typhoons or hurricanes.

Storms and weather systems develop circular patterns because of the Earth's rotation. Because the Earth has a solid surface, all points on its surface rotate once around in the same length of time. But points on the equator have farther to go in that time than do points at higher or lower latitudes. (The poles don't move at all.) A cloud moving northward or southward away from the equator has more forward motion than do other clouds at its new latitude. As a result, the cloud seems to be moving forward even faster. A spiral develops. The process is known as the Coriolis effect.

The Coriolis effect causes spiral weather patterns in many places. Close-up photographs from space have shown that Jupiter's Great Red Spot (see p. 59) and Neptune's Great Dark Spot have such spiral patterns. Storms on Mars have also been seen to spiral in this way.

A spiral storm over the Pacific Ocean, photographed from a space shuttle.

ıtes used to map the Earth include the ısat series of the United States, the SPOT ıes of the European Space Agency, and a oviet system. These satellites take photographs not only in the visible part of the spectrum — that is, with light our eyes can detect — but also in the infrared. Although we cannot see infrared (heat waves), infrared photographs show temperature well.

The photograph below shows Boston, Massachusetts, at the top; Providence, Rhode Island, at the center; and Cape Cod to the right. One infrared color has been reproduced as a false visible color along with two ordinary visible colors. In cities, the concrete, which radiates heat, makes urban areas appear quite different (bright blue) from rural areas, which have more plants (shown in red).

Photographs taken from space help in studying geology. For example, many lakes are long and skinny in the north-south direction. This reveals the direction in which melting glaciers moved as they scoured out the lakes tens of thousands of years ago.

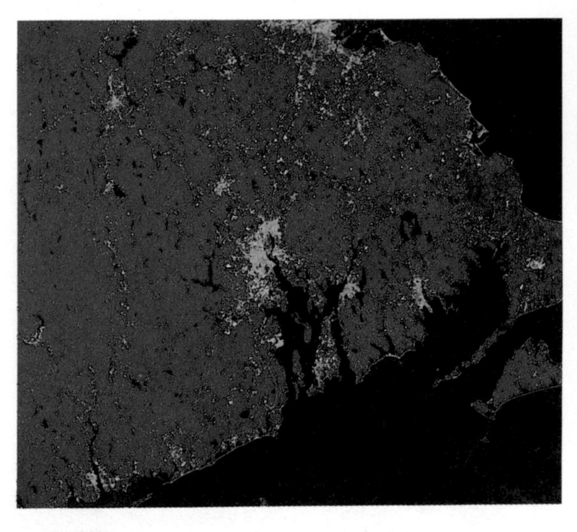

Parts of Massachusetts, Rhode Island, and Connecticut, shown in false color in this image taken with cameras on the Landsat 4 spacecraft.

Space mapping can be used for planning purposes. Here we see the region of New York City. As in the photo on p. 14, one infrared color has been reproduced in a false visible color. Urban areas are blue, and areas with trees and grass are red.

Manhattan Island extends upward (north) from the center of the view. In its midst is the rectangular Central Park, which appears reddish. Ships can be seen in New York Bay. Long Island extends to the right (east), with John F. Kennedy International Airport at its southern edge and LaGuardia Airport at its northern edge. The Bronx, to the north of Long Island and Manhattan, has many wooded areas, which also appear red. New Jersey is across the Hudson River to the west, joined to Manhattan by the George Washington Bridge. The Verrazano Narrows Bridge, at bottom center, joins Long Island (right) and Staten Island (left).

The Landsat spacecraft had a best resolution of 100 feet (30 meters). In other words, no details smaller than 100 feet across could be distinguished in the pictures it transmitted.

The New York City region, from the Landsat 4 spacecraft.

h

y phenomena studied on Earth can be nd or searched for on other planets. Scien- sts have discovered that the Earth has layers. ts top layer, the crust, slides on a semimelted layer below it. The continents are part of the crust. Over millions of years they have moved across the surface of the Earth, in a process known as *continental drift.*

The Earth's crust is divided into several plates. The study of the plates and how they move is known as plate tectonics. Two continental plates meet in California at the San Andreas Fault (see below). The plate containing Los Angeles is drifting northwest, and will one day bring Los Angeles north of San Francisco. In the meantime, a lot of energy is stored in geologic faults like this one when the plates are locked to each other. Occasionally, some of this energy is released in a devastating fashion as an earthquake.

Scientists plan to bounce radar waves (radar is short for "radio detection and ranging") from the Magellan spacecraft off the surface of Venus, to make more detailed maps of the planet's features. This process, known as high-resolution radar mapping, is expected to reveal whether Venus also has continental plates.

The San Andreas Fault in California, photographed from the air. The energy stored can be released as an earthquake when the continental plates on either side of this fault shift suddenly.

Volcanoes are one of many signs that Earth's interior is hot. Volcanoes often e near the boundaries of continental plates, sometimes exist as hot spots in the middle plate.

The Hawaiian Islands are formed from matter rising from a hot spot deep underground. As the drifting continental plate carrying the islands moves northwest, new islands are formed. Volcanic action then dies down on the older islands to the southeast.

Volcanoes act differently, depending on their gas content. Hawaiian volcanoes erupt more gently than do explosive ones such as Mount St. Helens.

Using spacecraft, scientists have discovered volcanoes on other planets and their moons. For example, giant volcanoes on Jupiter's moon Io (see p. 61) have been seen to erupt hundreds of miles into space. Huge volcanoes also appear on Mars. Some features on the surface of Venus seem to be giant volcanoes. Astronomers have detected material the volcanoes have erupted into Venus's atmosphere.

Kilauea Volcano erupting on Hawaii. We see fountains of lava (molten rock) rising to a height of 600 feet (200 meters).

The Moon

[illegible] moon is 2,160 miles (3,476 km) in diame- [illegible] about one-fourth the diameter of the [illegible]rth. If we could look down from a distant [illegible]ar, we would see the moon orbiting the [illegible]arth every $27\frac{1}{3}$ days, in a path slightly (less than 6%) out of round. The average distance from the Earth to the moon, center to center, is 239,000 miles (384,500 km).

As the moon moves around the Earth, the Earth continues to move in its orbit around the sun. Thus each time the moon makes one orbit around the Earth, as seen from a star, the Earth has moved ahead. It takes the moon an extra two days to catch up. The moon therefore takes about $29\frac{1}{2}$ days to reach the same position in our sky. (The period can range from $29\frac{1}{4}$ to $29\frac{3}{4}$ days.)

We see the moon go through phases every $29\frac{1}{2}$ days, as we see more or less of the half of the moon lighted by the sun. In the crescent phase (below), we see only a sliver that is lighted by the sun. The sun is almost behind the moon at this time, and the moon and sun appear close together in the sky. Thus the crescent moon always appears close to sunrise or sunset.

The crescent moon is only visible near sunrise or sunset.

Galileo discovered the surface features on the moon in 1610, when he first turned the newly invented telescope on it. He found that there are smooth, dark areas that look like seas, even though they contain no water. He named these lunar "seas" *maria* (pronounced "MAH-ree-ah"). Each one is a *mare* (pronounced "MAH-ray").

As the moon revolves around the Earth, it rotates on its axis so that the same half, more or less, always faces the Earth. Also, half the moon is always lighted by the sun, just as half of any round body is lighted by a faraway light. But the half that is lighted usually includes part of the moon that we can see and part that we never see. As the month goes on, the angle from the Earth to the moon to the sun changes, so different parts of the moon are lighted. The phase we see depends on how much of the lighted half of the moon is in the half of the moon that we see.

At the beginning of each monthly cycle, only the far side of the moon is lighted. We have a *new moon*. A century before Galileo, Leonardo da Vinci realized that even the dark part of the moon received some light from the sun that was bounced off the Earth to the moon. A new moon or the dark part of a crescent moon can sometimes be seen by this "earthshine."

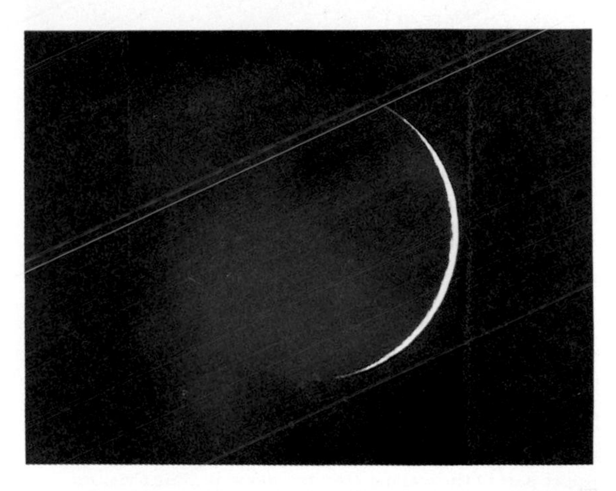

Just after the new moon, we see a thin crescent.

e Waxing Crescent

the Earth spins on its axis every 24 hours, e moon moves around the Earth in the same irection. For our view to catch up with the moon, the Earth must spin a little longer, usually 50 minutes. So the moon usually rises about 50 minutes later from night to night.

After the new moon, the crescent is not visible for a day or so. The time when the moon becomes visible depends on the weather: with perfectly clear skies, the moon is visible even in the daytime.

As we see more and more of the lighted half of the moon each night, we say the moon "waxes." The *waxing crescent* becomes visible in the evening sky near sunset, usually when the sky begins to darken. It sets a few hours after the sun.

Because of the moon's elliptical orbit around the Earth and because its orbit is tilted, we sometimes see more to one side or another around the moon's edge. These changes in angle, called *librations,* allow us to see slightly more than one-half of the moon over time. When the angle permits, we might see Mare Smythii — Smyth's Sea — on the crescent's edge.

The waxing crescent moon. The dark oval feature in the upper part of the waxing crescent moon is Mare Crisium, the Sea of Crises.

The First Quarter

A week after the new moon, we see the *first-quarter moon.* Half the face of the moon we se is lighted by the sun, so this phase is also known as a *half moon.* Now Mare Fecunditatis has become visible south of Mare Crisium. As the crescent waxes, we next see Mare Tranquillitatis, the Sea of Tranquillity. It is so flat and smooth that it was chosen, for safety reasons, as the site of the first human landing on the moon by the Apollo 11 astronauts Neil Armstrong and Buzz Aldrin in 1969.

The line dividing lighted from shadowed regions on the moon is called the *terminator.* Shadows are longest at the terminator, so craters and mountains stand out. Even from the Earth, we can calculate the heights of lunar mountains by measuring the heights of their shadows. The southern half of the visible side of the moon is covered with highlands.

Because the middle of the curved side of the quarter moon is facing the sun, we can tell from looking at the moon the direction toward the sun.

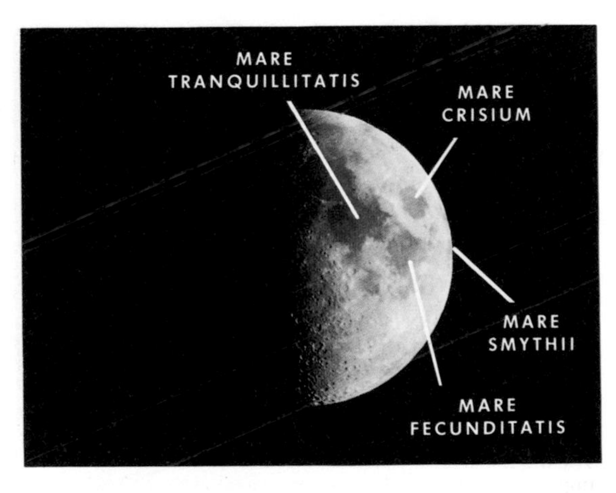

The first-quarter moon.

ꞁe Waxing Gibbous Moon

ʼhen the lunar phase is between quarter and .ull, we have a *gibbous moon.* (You can recall that a gibbous moon "gib us" — gives us — more light than a crescent or half moon does.) Prominent craters have become visible. The light-colored rays or streaks extending from the craters show us that these craters are relatively young — only millions of years old. Over time, the rays darken until they are indistinguishable from their surroundings.

In the highlands, in the southern hemisphere of the moon, is the rayed crater Tycho. Tycho was the 16th-century astronomer whose keen observations of the positions of the planets, before the telescope was invented, were precise enough to allow Johannes Kepler to discover the laws of planetary orbits.

In the northern hemisphere, in the midst of lunar seas, is the rayed crater Copernicus. Copernicus was the 17th-century astronomer who was the first person in the modern era to advance the theory that the sun, rather than the Earth, is at the center of the solar system. Rays from the crater Copernicus extend north into Mare Imbrium and south into Mare Nubium — the Sea of Clouds. The rayed crater Kepler comes into view a day or two after Copernicus is visible.

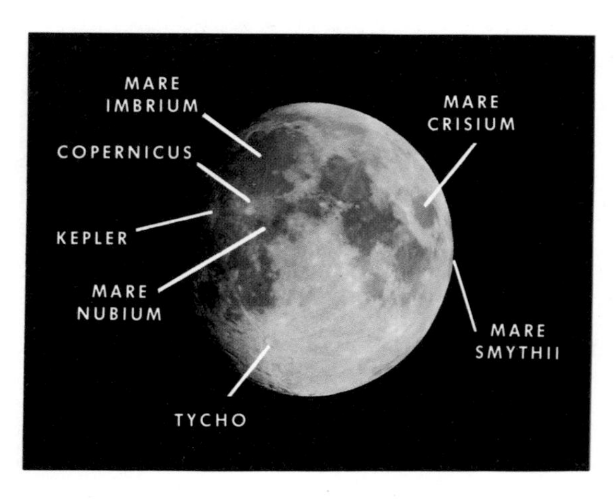

The waxing gibbous moon.

The Full Moon

About two weeks after a new moon, we have a *full moon*. Since the sun's light is hitting the center of the full moon straight on, we see little detail in the craters. It is a good time to view the lunar "seas."

The large mare (sea) near the northern half of the newly visible edge of the moon is Oceanus Procellarum. Together with Mare Imbrium and Mare Nubium, Oceanus Procellarum makes most of that quarter of the moon appear relatively dark.

Billions of years ago, lava flowed out from under the moon's surface to make the smooth maria, or lunar seas. The occasional craters on top of the maria have been made by more recent impacts of meteorites.

Because the moon's orbit around the Earth is tilted by 19° to 28°, the path the moon takes across the sky is sometimes a higher arc and sometimes a lower arc. When the arc is becoming higher above the horizon, the moon rises earlier than it otherwise would have. In the fall, this earlier rising offsets most of the time lag (50 minutes a night) in the moon's normal rising time. Thus in autumn, the moon — full or nearly so — rises at about the same time for a few nights. This phenomenon has long provided light for the harvest, and is known as the harvest moon.

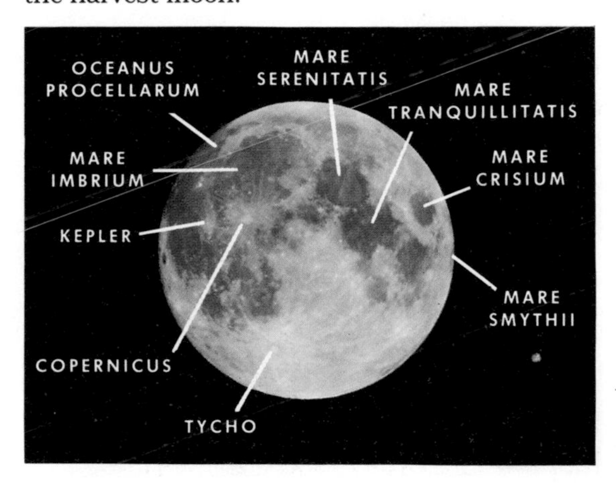

The full moon.

The Waning Gibbous Moon

The moon is said to be waning when it is past full and the lighted part appears to diminish from night to night. At the midpoint of the moon's edge is Grimaldi, officially a large, flat-bottomed crater but actually a small lunar sea. Lava has flowed across its bottom, making it appear as dark as the maria.

The rayed crater Tycho, in the southern half of the moon, remains the most prominent feature. To its south is the largest crater on the moon, Clavius. It is 140 miles (225 km) in diameter, about the size of Massachusetts.

Since the full moon occurs when the moon is opposite the sun in the sky, the full moon rises at sunset. Thus the *waning gibbous moon* rises after sunset, about 50 minutes later each night. It is then visible through the rest of the night. It is, of course, also visible during the morning daylight if the sky is sufficiently clear and free of haze.

The waning gibbous phase is a good time to use binoculars to look back at the terminator (line between light and dark) as it crosses the features you saw at the waxing crescent. Make sketches to compare the two views.

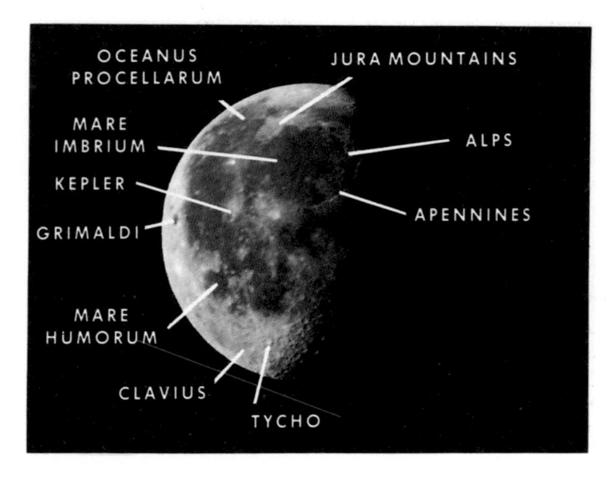

The waning gibbous moon.

The Third Quarter

The *third-quarter moon* rises at midnight. Though the terminator — division between light and dark — is in the same location as it was for the first-quarter moon, the craters are illuminated from the opposite side. The rayed craters Tycho, Copernicus, and Kepler remain prominent.

The moon in this phase sets at noon, after it has been visible, in clear weather, throughout the morning. Following the third-quarter moon, the moon rises after midnight and is visible only in the wee hours before sunrise or in daylight hours. Thus the *waning crescent* is seen less often than other phases.

As the moon wanes past third quarter, the terminator crosses many interesting features. The Jura Mountains above Mare Imbrium, due north of the crater Copernicus, are but one of several examples of mountain ranges on the moon that are named after mountain ranges on Earth (see photo, p. 24). A detailed map of the moon, showing many craters, mountain ranges, maria, and so on, appears in *A Field Guide to the Stars and Planets.*

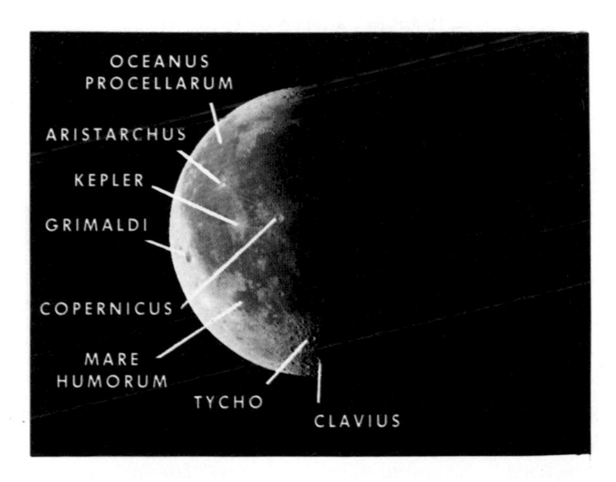

The third-quarter moon.

Lunar Eclipses

At the full moon, the sun is behind the Earth, casting its sunlight over our shoulders directly onto the moon. But because the moon's orbit is tilted, the Earth's shadow usually misses covering the moon. Every few months, though, the sun, Earth, and moon are right in line, and we have a lunar eclipse.

A lunar eclipse takes up to a few hours. First, we see the round shadow of the Earth gradually cover more and more of the moon's surface. During a *partial lunar eclipse*, this partial covering is all that occurs. Sometimes, when the alignment of the sun, Earth, and moon is even more exact, the moon goes entirely into the Earth's dark shadow. A *total lunar eclipse* results.

During a total lunar eclipse, no light reaches the moon directly from the sun, because the Earth is in the way. However, some sunlight is bent around the Earth by our atmosphere. Usually only the red part of the sun's light gets through our atmosphere; the rest of the light makes skies blue on Earth. Thus during a total lunar eclipse, the moon sometimes glows faintly reddish (see below). When there is a lot of dust in the Earth's atmosphere, the moon's faint glow is more grayish.

Anybody on Earth can see a lunar eclipse if the moon is above their horizon at that time and the sky is clear. Dates of total lunar eclipses visible in the United States and Canada during 1990–2000 are December 9, 1992 (eastern); June 4, 1993 (western); November 29, 1993; April 4, 1996 (eastern); and September 27, 1996.

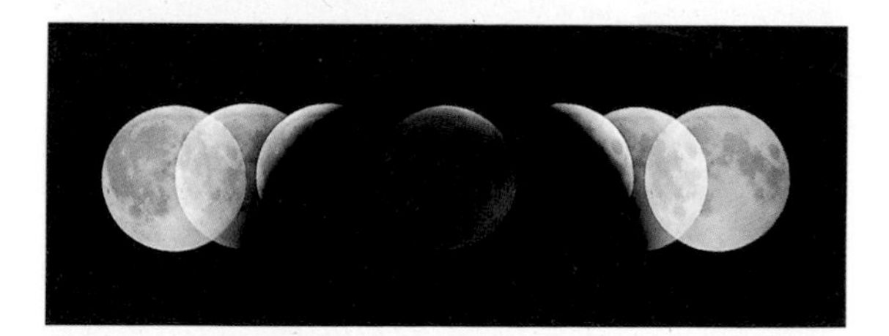

This multiple exposure shows how the moon moves through the Earth's shadow during a lunar eclipse. The shape of the Earth's shadow proves that the Earth is round.

Landing on the Moon

Between 1969 and 1972, six American spac craft, each carrying two astronauts, landed o the moon. The first human to land was Neil Armstrong, aboard Apollo 11. The first words he said when he set foot on the moon were, "One small step for man, one giant leap for mankind." (He had practiced saying "One small step for a man," but made a mistake.)

Astronauts aboard the several Apollo missions carried out many experiments on the moon. For example, they placed seismometers to listen for moonquakes. After the astronauts departed, these instruments radioed back reports of moonquakes to Earth. The reports enabled scientists to discover that the moon's interior is hot and melted, like Earth's.

Mirrors the astronauts left on the moon are still being used to reflect laser beams back to Earth. This helps scientists measure the distance between the Earth and the moon very accurately.

The astronauts carried back 843 pounds (382 kilograms) of rocks from the moon to Earth. Scientists in laboratories on Earth analyzed the rocks to figure out their ages. The oldest rocks were 4.42 billion years old, which must be when the moon's surface solidified.

In one of the most famous pictures of the space age, astronaut Buzz Aldrin walks on the moon. The photograph was taken by the only other person on the moon that day, Neil Armstrong.

onauts on the Moon

astronauts traveled to the moon in a Com-
and Module, with a smaller Lunar Module
ttached. The Command Module went into
orbit around the moon. One astronaut, Michael Collins, remained aboard the Command Module while the other two, Buzz Aldrin and Neil Armstrong, landed on the moon.

Here we see the view from the Command Module while the Lunar Module began its landing. The rough surface of the moon is below. Note the shallow craters in the foreground and the lunar mountains in the distance and along the moon's horizon.

Photographs the astronauts took of the far side of the moon revealed its surface clearly for the first time. The far side is heavily cratered. Unlike the side nearest the Earth, it has few maria (lunar seas).

The Lunar Module during its descent for a lunar landing. The Earth is visible in the sky. Its blue image stands in contrast to the barrenness of the lunar surface.

Astronauts on the Moon

The Apollo 11 astronauts landed on a smooth part of Mare Tranquillitatis. They stayed on the moon for only a few hours. By the last Apollo mission, the astronauts had landed in rougher, rockier regions, and even had a little car that allowed them to travel on the moon for several miles. They tried to collect as many different types of rocks as possible, in order to help understand the formation of the moon and its surface.

Studies of the rocks the astronauts brought back from the moon showed that the lunar surface was bombarded by meteorites between about 4.2 and 3.9 billion years ago. Then hot lava from inside the moon flowed out onto the lunar surface, covering and smoothing the regions we now call maria (lunar seas). This volcanic activity took place more than 3.1 billion years ago. The moon has changed little since then.

Scientists now think that the moon may have formed when a large object collided with the Earth. Material was ejected into orbit around the Earth, and eventually collected under the force of its own gravity to make the moon. Scientists had hoped that studying the moon would show them material from the earliest years of the solar system. But the discovery that the moon's surface had melted billions of years ago dashed that hope. Now we look to comets (see p. 104) to take us farther back in time.

Apollo 17 astronaut Harrison Schmidt, the only scientist who ever landed on the moon, examining a huge lunar boulder. The Lunar Rover he drove is at right.

Mercury

Mercury, the innermost planet, orbits very close to the sun. Anyone watching it from Earth will never see it stray far from the sun in our sky. Mercury is not bright enough to be visible in the daytime, except during a total solar eclipse; it can be seen only near sunrise or sunset, usually low in the sky. At those times we are looking at a slant through the Earth's atmosphere. Because this slanted path passes through a lot of moving air, images we get of Mercury are always blurred.

For a few nights in a row, two or three times a year, we can see Mercury in the evening sky, weather permitting. It can be as bright as the brightest star. A telescope would reveal that it goes through a series of phases, but the planet's disk is too small for us to see the phases with the eye or with ordinary binoculars.

Mercury is, on average, 36 million miles (58 million km) from the sun — 40% of the distance of the Earth from the sun. However, Mercury's orbit is not round; in fact, it is much farther out of round than that of the Earth or of any of the other planets except Pluto. At times, Mercury is much closer to the sun — it can be as close as 29 million miles (47 million km), or as far away as 43 million miles (70 million km).

Mercury in the sky at twilight, near the crescent moon.

Mercury is so difficult to study from the Earth that for a long time astronomers didn't even know how long it takes Mercury to rotate on its axis, the length of one of Mercury's days. Finally, radar waves bounced off Mercury showed that the planet rotates in 59 days, as seen from our bird's-eye position over the solar system. This is two-thirds of the time it takes to revolve around the sun.

A point on the daylight side of Mercury receives sunlight for so long and from such a close distance that the maximum temperature reaches over 400°C (800°F). Mercury has practically no atmosphere to spread the energy around the planet. Traces of sodium making a very thin atmosphere around Mercury were discovered fairly recently. But for the most part, sunlight gives particles near Mercury so much energy that they escape from Mercury's weak gravity.

There are no moons around Mercury. Photographs of the region around the planet would have shown a moon even if it were as small as 3 miles (about 5 km) across.

Much of what we know about Mercury comes from a single spacecraft — NASA's Mariner 10, which visited Mercury in 1974 and 1975. Cameras on board showed that Mercury is mostly covered with craters (see below). Other instruments showed that Mercury is covered with fine dust and that it has a small magnetic field.

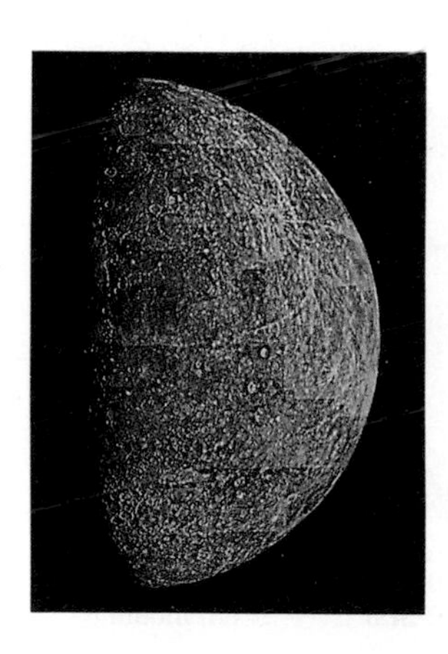

A mosaic of Mercury, made of photographs taken by Mariner 10. The planet's north pole is near the top.

Mercury

Although Mercury receives a great deal of light from the sun, the planet's surface is really fairly dark, reflecting only 6% of the sunlight that hits it. Mercury appears bright in the sky to us only because we are seeing it against the even darker background of the sky.

At first sight, Mercury looks much like the Earth's moon. Craters with bright rays are one of several kinds of features they have in common. Some of the craters are 125 miles (200 km) in diameter. But craters on Mercury, on closer examination, are shallower than those on the moon. They also have thinner rims.

Radar observations made from Earth are continuing the studies of craters. These new observations allow scientists to study the side of Mercury that was not studied by the Mariner 10 spacecraft.

Mercury has major lines of cliffs, known, as on Earth, as scarps. The scarp shown below, near Mercury's edge, is hundreds of miles long. The scarps apparently formed when Mercury contracted as it cooled, not long after it was formed. The cooling wrinkled the planet's surface.

A collision with another object soon after it was formed may have stripped off the outermost parts of Mercury. The oldest of Mercury's features that we see were probably formed 4.2 billion years ago. Mercury has some regions of smooth plains, which were formed at least 3.8 billion years ago.

A Mariner 10 view across 365 miles (580 km) of Mercury, showing a long scarp near the edge.

By international agreement, the International Astronomical Union assigns names to newly discovered features in the solar system. Mercury's plains have been named after Mercury in different languages, such as Suisui in Japanese, Tir in Persian, and Odin in Norwegian. Craters on Mercury have been named for authors, composers, and artists; the names of scientists are assigned, by contrast, to craters on our moon.

Ten times since 1900, Mercury has gone "in transit" across the sun, as seen from Earth. At these times, Mercury looks like a tiny black dot on the sun's disk. The transit of November 6, 1993, will be visible from Europe but not from North America. The transit of November 15, 1999, will be visible only from the very southernmost part of Earth. Not until May 7, 2003, will a transit of Mercury again be visible from North America. *Never look directly at the sun* — special protective solar filters are necessary to observe the sun and a transit safely.

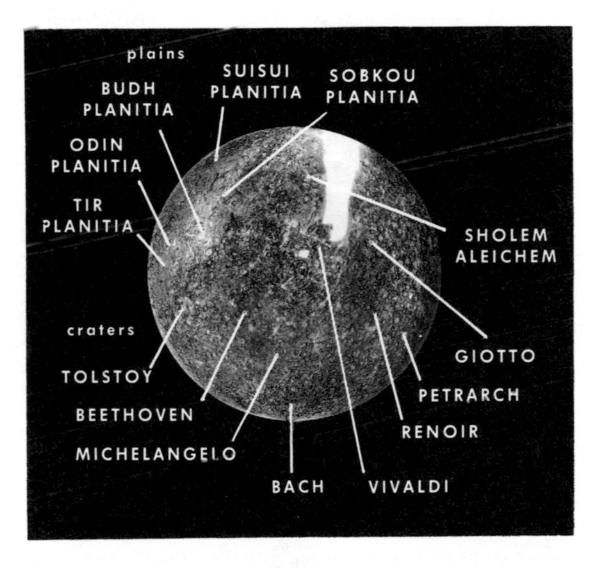

An airbrushed map of the side of Mercury observed from Mariner 10.

Venus

Venus comes nearer to Earth than any other planet. Since it is both relatively close to the sun and reflects most of the sun's light because of its cloud cover, it appears very bright in our sky. Venus can be the brightest object in the sky aside from the sun and the moon. It can even be bright enough to cast shadows.

Venus's orbit is 70% of the radius of the Earth's orbit, or about two-thirds of the distance from the sun to the Earth. Though Venus is never very far from the sun in our sky, it can be as much as 45° away — a distance you can estimate by holding four or five fists at arm's length against the sky. At those times Venus rises as much as three hours before the sun does and sets as much as three hours after the sun sets.

When Venus rises before the sun and gleams brightly in the morning sky, it is called the *morning star.* When Venus sets after the sun and gleams brightly in the evening sky, it is called the *evening star.*

When Venus is low in the sky, the light from it to us passes low over much of the Earth. It crosses so many rising air currents that the image of the planet is often distorted. The distortion can be different for different colors, so Venus can seem to be turning red and green.

Venus as the evening star along with the crescent moon. A telescope with sufficient magnification would show that Venus is also in a crescent phase (see p. 35) at this time.

Venus goes through a full set of phases. When it is a crescent it is nearer to us than the sun, so it appears larger than when it is gibbous. Galileo discovered that Venus goes through a full set of phases, and that its image changes in size in this manner. This was a major proof in the 17th century that Copernicus was correct in saying that the sun, rather than the Earth, is at the center of the solar system.

The naked eye or binoculars do not show the phases of Venus, but even small telescopes do. It is interesting to follow the change in size and phase of Venus over a six-month period.

Twice each century or so, Venus goes in transit across the face of the sun. The two transits are separated by only eight years. The next pair of transits will be on June 8, 2004, and June 5–6, 2012. When Captain Cook sailed to the south seas to observe the 1769 transit of Venus across the sun, he discovered Australia and New Zealand as bonuses.

From Earth, we can see the phases of Venus, but clouds on the planet prevent us from seeing its surface.

Venus's Atmosphere

The clouds of Venus allow sunlight to pass through. The sunlight heats Venus's surface, which gives off mainly infrared rays. Unlike sunlight, these infrared rays cannot pass up and out through the clouds. The energy of the infrared radiation is thus trapped by the atmosphere of Venus, and the planet heats up. The process is known as the "greenhouse effect."

We have a greenhouse effect on Earth, too. The greenhouse effect we now have is about 20°C (35°F) of warming, enough to make the Earth a comfortable planet for us. But we have recently realized that as we continue to burn fossil fuels such as coal and oil, we are adding so much carbon dioxide to the Earth's atmosphere that the amount of greenhouse warming we will have is increasing. We worry about changing weather patterns and about flooding of coasts as Arctic and Antarctic ice melts and oceans rise. Studies of Venus have shown us how important it is to preserve our Earth.

We are also learning more about the chemistry of our Earth's atmosphere from studying Venus's. We realize that the protective layer of ozone in the upper part of the Earth's atmosphere is being depleted, which allows more ultraviolet light to enter.

A view of Venus in a crescent phase, taken with a telescope on Earth. This infrared view shows the infrared radiation (often called "heat rays") from the unlighted side of Venus.

From outside the Earth's atmosphere, we can use ultraviolet light to photograph Venus. These photographs show structure in Venus's clouds. Though Venus rotates *very* slowly — each rotation takes 229 Earth days — the clouds move around Venus very quickly.

The clouds contain droplets of sulfuric acid. Venus's atmosphere is 95% carbon dioxide, compared with less than 0.1% carbon dioxide in Earth's atmosphere. Venus's atmosphere is at very high pressure. The pressure at the surface of Venus is almost 100 times higher than the air pressure at the Earth's surface.

Several spacecraft have studied the clouds of Venus. First, Mariner 10 took pictures of the clouds as it passed Venus en route to Mercury. Since 1979, NASA's Pioneer Venus mission has been in orbit around Venus.

The two Soviet Vega missions en route to Halley's Comet passed Venus in 1985 and released a balloon into Venus's atmosphere. The helium-filled balloons moved thousands of miles across Venus in very strong winds, measured at 150 miles (250 km) per hour.

Venus, from NASA's Pioneer Venus Orbiter. Bright clouds wrap around the poles, and a Y-shaped region of clouds covers much of the region around the planet's equator.

Venus Landers

Another Pioneer Venus mission carried four probes that traveled through Venus's atmosphere down to its surface. Winds near the surface were not as strong as those at higher altitudes.

The Soviet Union has built several robot spacecraft that have parachuted onto Venus and survived on its surface for up to about two hours. Some of these spacecraft have radioed back pictures. Venus's sky is orange, which adds an orange cast to the pictures. The surface around the landers is covered with flat rocks (see photo below).

The landers have analyzed some of the rocks, and found that they resemble basalt, a common type of rock on Earth that comes from volcanoes. At some sites on Venus, the rocks seem to have eroded more than sharp-edged rocks from other sites. Because the wind speed near the surface of Venus is low, the erosion may be caused mainly by melting or other temperature or chemical changes.

Venus's surface, photographed from the Soviet Venera 13 lander. Because of the way the image was scanned, the horizon appears slanted at upper right.

Venus's Surface (Radar Views)

Several spacecraft orbiting Venus have carried radars on board. These radars have sent pulses of radio waves down to Venus's surface; the radio waves were able to penetrate the clouds. Scientists have used the time it took for the waves to return to the spacecraft to calculate how high mountains and other features are. They have used the strength of the radio waves that bounced back to calculate the roughness of the planet's surface.

NASA's Pioneer Venus Orbiter has made a relief map of nearly the whole surface of Venus. Only features larger than 10 to 50 miles (about 20 to 100 km) across could be shown. Venus turns out to be almost entirely covered with a single rolling plain. Although the highest regions on Venus resemble continents, no signs of drifting continental plates are visible.

The high regions of Venus were named after the Greek goddess Aphrodite and the Babylonian goddess Ishtar, both counterparts of Venus, the Roman goddess of love.

The surface of Venus. Different heights have been color-coded, based on radar mapping from the Pioneer Venus spacecraft. The regions shown in red, brown, and yellow are the highest areas. The map shows one continent, named Aphrodite Terra, near the planet's equator, and another continent, Ishtar Terra, at higher latitudes.

Venus

Radar data from the Pioneer Venus Orbiter were used to make detailed maps of the highest regions on Venus, which resemble continents on Earth. The largest continent, Ishtar Terra, has a high mountain named Maxwell, which is up to 7 miles (11 km) high. Ishtar Terra (see p. 39) is about the size of the United States.

Close to Venus's equator is the continent Aphrodite Terra. It is twice as large as Ishtar and much more rugged.

Other features on Venus's surface appear to be giant volcanoes. Studies of Venus's atmosphere have also shown changes in the level of certain gases that seem to show that volcanoes are currently active on Venus. The level of sulfur dioxide, for example, went up drastically between visits of different spacecraft.

Also on Venus is a giant canyon, almost as long as the distance from New York to Georgia.

The lowlands cover only 16% of Venus, though they are similar to Earth's ocean basins, which cover most of Earth.

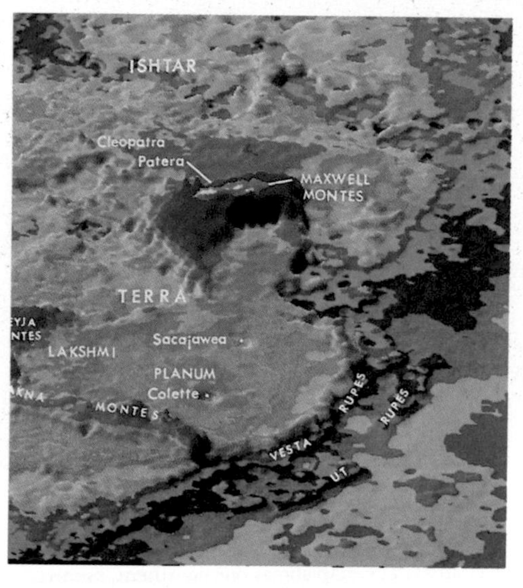

A detailed view of part of Ishtar Terra, based on radar data from Pioneer Venus.

Magellan Maps Venus

The Magellan spacecraft was launched from Earth in 1989, and is scheduled to reach Venus in 1990. Its radar is of a special design that should be able to map most of Venus's surface with a resolution of only 500 to 1,500 feet (200 to 500 meters). This amount of detail is 100 times finer than the resolution of our current Pioneer Venus radar map.

We hope that the radar map from Magellan will show lava flows or other fine features that will allow us to understand Venus's surface. We may even be able to see changes in the planet's surface over the period of time that Magellan is in orbit.

Some regions of Venus can be studied by radar from Earth. The giant radio telescope at Arecibo in Puerto Rico has been used to map these regions in finer detail than the maps made by previous U.S. and Soviet spacecraft. The Magellan spacecraft will use radar to help scientists make maps that will show still more detail.

Though Venus is often called Earth's sister planet because it is almost the same size and has almost the same mass, we now know of many ways in which Earth and Venus differ. Venus rotates much more slowly and has no moon. It has neither drifting continental plates nor a magnetic field in its crust. It has no water in its atmosphere, and it has a very high surface temperature.

The Magellan spacecraft, en route to Venus with its radar that should reveal much detail of the planet's surface structure.

Mars

Mars, the red planet, is visibly ruddy in our nighttime sky. Mars is smaller than Earth; its diameter is only about one-half (53%) of the Earth's diameter and it contains only one-tenth the Earth's mass. The radius of Mars' orbit is one and one-half times the distance from the sun to Earth. Since Mars orbits the sun outside the Earth's orbit, it can be on the opposite side of the Earth from the sun. At such times, it is at *opposition* and can be viewed all night long.

Mars' orbit is 9% out of round, so it is closer to Earth at some oppositions than at others. It can be as large as 1⁄75 the diameter of the full moon and as small as 1⁄130 the diameter. When Mars is at opposition, it can be one of the brightest objects in the sky, but otherwise it is not so noticeable. Its reddish color matches that of some of the stars, notably Aldebaran and Antares, whose name means "compared with Mars."

Usually Mars moves slightly ahead of the stars in the sky from night to night, but as the Earth passes Mars, Mars appears to move backward. These *retrograde loops* in the planet's orbit show clearly in the maps of Mars' position that begin on p. 52.

During the opposition of 1988, Mars came as close to the Earth as it ever does, and was so bright that it could be seen in the sky even from the center of a city. Here we see the bright dot of Mars and, at left, the overexposed moon in clouds.

Mars from the Ground

Mars' disk, or apparent "face" in the sky, is too small to show much detail to small telescopes. Astronomers have examined Mars in detail with large telescopes for over a century. Dark, greenish regions cover part of Mars' surface. These areas cover more of Mars during the martian "springtime," which comes at different times in Mars' northern or southern hemisphere. (As it orbits the sun, Mars is tilted on its axis at about the same angle as the Earth, so it also has seasons.) During spring and summer in Mars' northern hemisphere, that half of the planet is tilted toward the sun, and receives the sun's rays more directly.

Many decades ago, it was thought that the spreading greenish regions might be vegetation growing on Mars. Furthermore, there were reports of long features on Mars that were mistranslated from Italian as "canals." As a result, people wondered whether there were living things on Mars. We now know that the greenish regions appear to spread because reddish dust is blown off them by martian winds. And we know that the "canals" were mere optical illusions. There is no evidence of life on Mars.

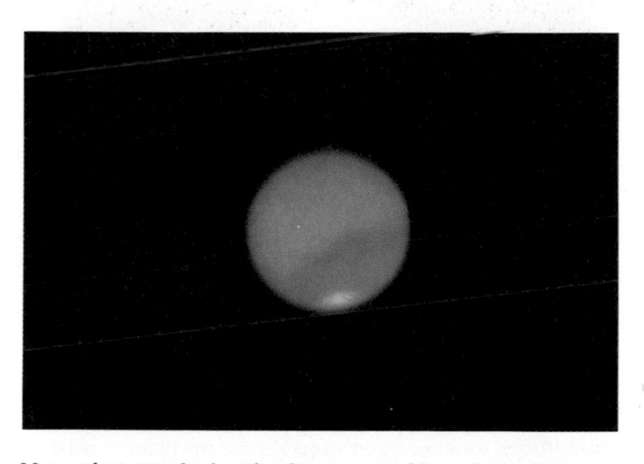

Mars, photographed with a large ground-based telescope. The darkest region, shaped like Africa, is Syrtis Major. The horizontal strip to the right is Sinus Sabaeus.

Mars from the Ground

New techniques allow astronomers to make the best use of Mars' close oppositions with Earth. Ground-based sensors at the 1988 opposition (which was very close) picked up more detail on Mars than ever before. There is no sign that the "canals" on Mars exist. Apparently, the human eye and brain merely connected markings on the planet that weren't really linked.

Mars has polar caps that vary with the seasons. They wax and wane each martian year, which lasts 780 Earth days, or two Earth years and two months. The polar caps turn out to be mostly carbon dioxide — "dry ice." When the carbon dioxide disappears during the summertime in one hemisphere or the other on Mars, a residual polar cap of water ice remains. Though no signs of life exist on Mars, the presence of water gives hope to those who still want to search (see p. 50).

Mars' surface dust is reddish because of iron oxides — rust — in it. The exact chemical form is not known.

Dust storms on Mars can be studied from Earth. Amateur astronomers keep track of them.

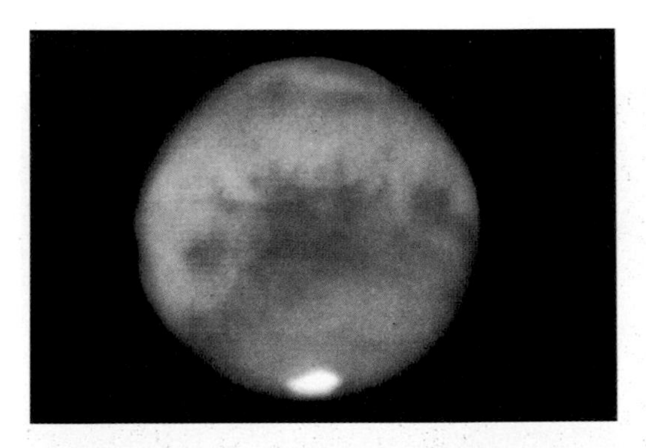

An image of Mars during the September 1988 opposition. The white cap of carbon dioxide ("dry ice") is clearly visible on the planet's south pole, along with the blue-white hood of frost (frozen water or water vapor) above the planet's north pole. The blue-white veils at the east and west are from haze in Mars' atmosphere. Sinus Aurorae is in the center and Sinus Meridiani is the feature near the right edge.

Mars from Viking

In 1976, NASA's two Viking spacecraft reached Mars. Each contained an orbiting part and a lander. The orbiters discovered many types of features on the martian surface.

The martian volcanoes are quite spectacular. In the photograph above, plumes of clouds containing water ice trail from the giant volcano Ascraeus Mons. Extending downward in the middle of the crescent Mars in the photo is a huge series of valleys. These are named Valles Marineris, which means "Mariner Valleys," after the NASA spacecraft that visited Mars on an earlier mission. Argyre, a large crater, is visible at the bottom of the image, and the region is covered with frost. Mars' south pole is at the bottom of the photograph.

The Viking orbiters sent back more than 50,000 pictures of Mars to scientists on Earth. Neither orbiter is still working. The orbiters photographed spiral cloud patterns that are similar to storms on Earth. Studies of the weather on Mars are helping us understand our own weather systems on Earth. We now realize that dust storms in the African deserts, for example, put dust into the air that we detect in the United States.

Dawn on Mars, photographed by Viking Orbiter 2 as it approached Mars.

Mars from Viking

An image transmitted as Viking 1 approached Mars showed that one whole part of the planet was covered with giant volcanoes. The largest is Olympus Mons, Mount Olympus, visible at upper right. Scientists think that the absence of continental drift on Mars leaves volcanoes in the same place, where they can continue to grow and grow. Volcanoes on Earth, on the other hand, eventually move off their underground sources and do not become as large.

Mars' atmosphere is much thinner than Earth's, with about 1/100 the pressure at Mars' surface. Still, the atmosphere is visible at the edge of Mars, as a whitish rim. The atmosphere is 90% carbon dioxide, with small amounts of nitrogen and argon and traces of carbon monoxide, oxygen, and water vapor.

Mars' surface shows stream beds with tributaries, as though water once flowed in them.

Scientists can figure out the relative ages of some features on Mars by noting what covers what. For example, if a crater is seen in a stream bed, then the stream bed must have been there when the crater was formed. Only when spacecraft land on Mars and either carry instruments that can date rocks or bring rocks back to Earth will we have absolute dates for the age of martian rocks.

Mars, from the Viking 1 spacecraft, showing the ridge of volcanoes.

Mars Mosaic

In the years since the Viking missions, the thousands of photographs transmitted have been carefully studied on Earth.

Across the center, the Valles Marineris canyon complex extends 3,000 miles (5,000 km), the distance across the United States from coast to coast. This canyon system is thus much larger than Earth's Grand Canyon. Valles Marineris is up to 50 miles (80 km) across and its cliffs can be 5 miles (8 km) high. Noctis Labyrinthus is at its left.

The three volcanoes (at left) are from top to bottom, Ascraeus Mons, Pavonis Mons, and Arsia Mons. The tallest is 10 miles (17 km) above the surrounding plains — twice as tall as Earth's Mt. Everest is above sea level. Olympus Mons (see p. 48) is still larger.

Computers were used to piece together this mosaic of images of Mars, taken from the Viking 1 orbiter.

Olympus Mons

Mars' largest volcano, Olympus Mons, was discovered at the site of a feature seen from Earth, Nix Olympica, which means "the Snow of Olympus." Olympus was the residence of the gods in Greek mythology.

Olympus Mons is huge — 375 miles (600 km) across at its base and 15 miles (25 km) high, about three times as high as Earth's Mt. Everest. Clouds are often seen around the lower levels of Olympus Mons. Lava flows extend down its flanks. Its crater is 40 miles (65 km) wide; Manhattan Island would fit inside.

Volcanoes with gently sloping sides like the ones on Mars are called "shield volcanoes." The Hawaiian Islands are examples on Earth of shield volcanoes. Olympus Mons, though, is three times higher and five times wider than any volcano on Earth.

Scientists wonder why so many volcanoes are found in such a limited region of Mars. Perhaps Mars is still heating up from the radioactive elements in its interior and the volcanism will spread over time.

A false-color view of Olympus Mons. The region shown is just over 375 miles (600 km) wide.

Viking Lander Views of Mars

Two identical Viking landers descended on Mars during the summer of 1976. Each carried a color camera and a weather station. Temperatures at Mars' surface ranged from a high of 30°C (80°F) to a low of −125°C (−190°F).

The landers took about 4,500 pictures. One surprise they revealed was the pinkish sky on Mars. With hindsight, we realize that the sky is pinkish on Mars because of all the reddish dust in it. On Earth, on the other hand, the sky is blue because air scatters the blue part of sunlight (which contains all colors) better than it scatters the redder parts.

Mars' surface is covered with rocks. The rocks have the same appearance as volcanic rocks on Earth. The Viking 1 lander is on Chryse Planitia, a relatively smooth plain. The Viking 2 lander is on Utopia Planitia, a more northern plain, chosen because it was closer to the pole and therefore the spacecraft had a greater chance of finding water and perhaps life there. Viking 2 did find a higher proportion of water vapor in the atmosphere of that region of Mars.

View of Mars from the Viking 2 lander. One of the lander's footpads is resting on a rock, so the horizon appears tilted. The horizon is 2 miles (3 km) away. Wouldn't it be nice to have a rover that could see what is over the horizon?

The Search for Life on Mars

Each Viking lander carried a box packed with biology experiments designed to detect signs of life on Mars. In some of the experiments, the soil was mixed with liquids containing substances that would encourage growth. In another, the soil was heated to a high temperature to see which gases would escape. All the results can be matched by experiments using chemicals on Earth, and so they do not show that there is life on Mars. Another instrument examined molecules in the soil and found no organic ones. On Earth, even after plants or animals die, organic molecules are left.

Evidence from the polar caps and the stream beds that water may exist on Mars leaves many people still interested in further searches for life on Mars. Perhaps some of the water is buried underground as permafrost. Perhaps there were periods in the past when water flowed plentifully over Mars' surface. There is still plenty to search for on Mars, either with robot missions in the 1990s or missions with astronauts; the first manned mission could come no earlier than 2010.

A Viking lander on Mars. We see an arm that dug martian soil and placed it in a hopper.

The Moons of Mars

Mars has two tiny moons. Phobos, the larger moon, is only 17 miles (27 km) across. Deimos is only 9 miles (15 km) across. Phobos (which means "fear") and Deimos (which means "terror") are named after the companions of Ares, the Greek god of war. (Mars was the Roman god of war.)

Neither Phobos nor Deimos is round. They do not have enough gravity to pull them into a round shape. They may be asteroids (see p. 116) that have been captured with Mars' gravity. Further evidence that Phobos and Deimos were once asteroids comes from their color, which is very dark and which matches that of one type of asteroid.

The largest two craters on Phobos are named for Asaph Hall and his wife Angelina Stickney. Hall discovered the moons over 100 years ago.

Photographs were taken of both moons from the Viking spacecraft. In 1989, one of the Soviet Phobos missions reached Mars. Unfortunately, just before it was supposed to hover near Phobos and examine it at close range, contact with the spacecraft was lost. Several space missions to study Mars and its moons are planned.

Phobos and Deimos are too small and faint to be readily seen from Earth.

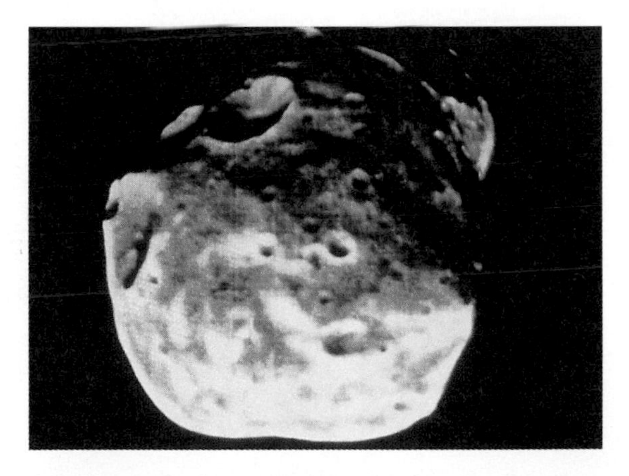

Phobos, from the Soviet Phobos mission.

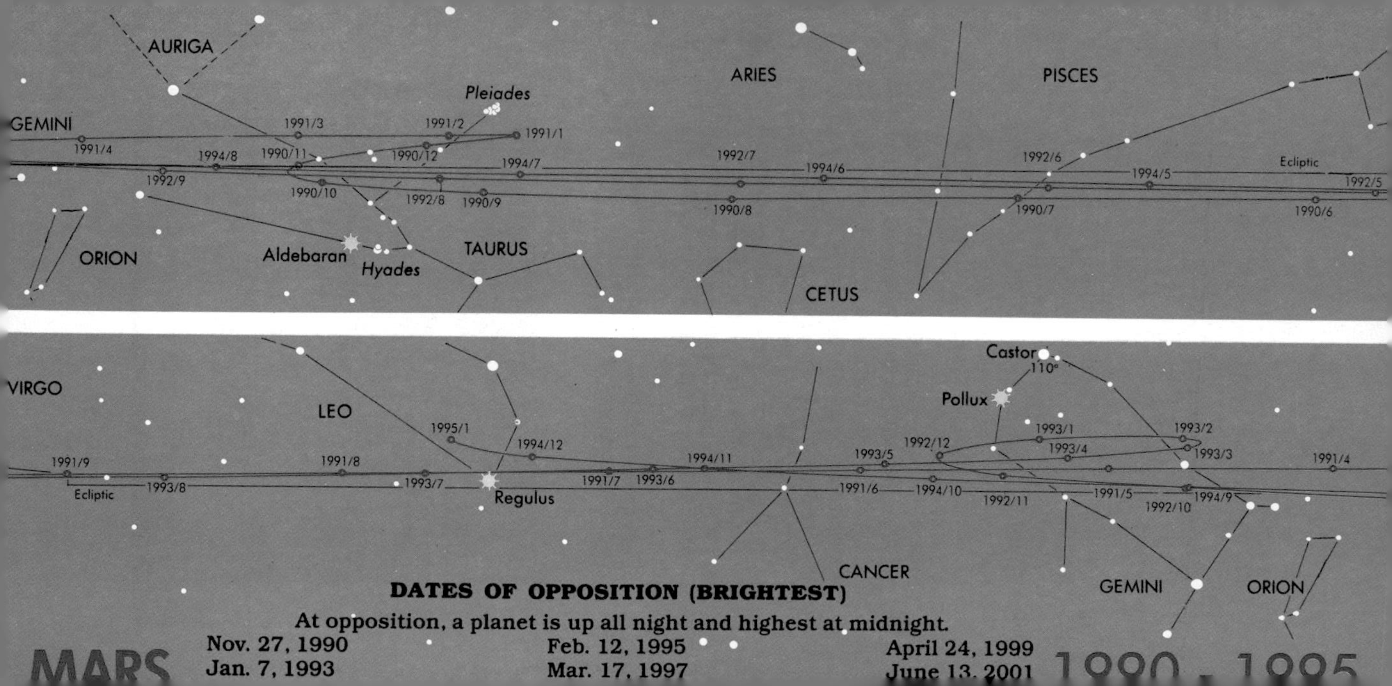
AURIGA
GEMINI
Pleiades
ARIES
PISCES
ORION
Aldebaran
Hyades
TAURUS
CETUS
Ecliptic
1991/4
1991/3
1991/2
1991/1
1994/8
1990/11
1990/12
1994/7
1992/7
1994/6
1992/6
1994/5
1992/5
1992/9
1990/10
1992/8
1990/9
1990/8
1990/7
1990/6
VIRGO
LEO
Castor
110°
Pollux
1995/1
1994/12
1991/9
1991/8
1993/8
1993/7
Regulus
1991/7
1993/6
1994/11
1993/5
1992/12
1993/1
1993/4
1993/2
1993/3
1991/4
1991/6
1994/10
1992/11
1991/5
1992/10
1994/9
CANCER
GEMINI
ORION
DATES OF OPPOSITION (BRIGHTEST)
At opposition, a planet is up all night and highest at midnight.
Nov. 27, 1990
Jan. 7, 1993
Feb. 12, 1995
Mar. 17, 1997
April 24, 1999
June 13, 2001
MARS 1990 - 1995

Jupiter's Ring

One of many surprising discoveries that the Voyager missions made about Jupiter was the existence of a ring around the planet. Jupiter's ring is much less spectacular than Saturn's, and is not visible from the Earth. But the spacecraft did discover one wispy narrow ring.

After the ring was discovered from Voyager 1, Voyager 2 got better images of it by looking back through the ring toward the sun. The way the particles in the ring scattered light showed that they were extremely tiny — only one-thousandth of a millimeter in size. Fainter material extends down from the ring to Jupiter's surface. The ring particles may have come from Io or been knocked off other inner moons. Another possibility is that they are debris from a meteor or a comet.

The Voyagers each made only one trip through the Jupiter system. NASA's Galileo spacecraft is scheduled to reach Jupiter and its moons in 1995. Galileo will drop a probe into Jupiter's atmosphere which will radio data back to Earth for an hour as the probe falls through the atmosphere.

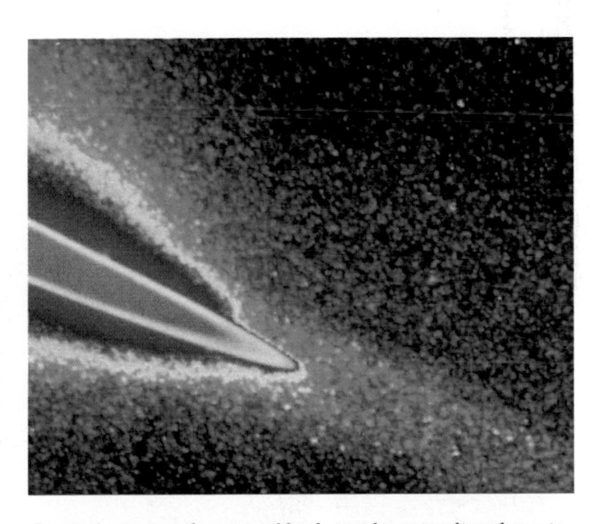

Jupiter's ring, with material both inside, extending down to Jupiter's surface, and outside the main ring, in a "gossamer ring."

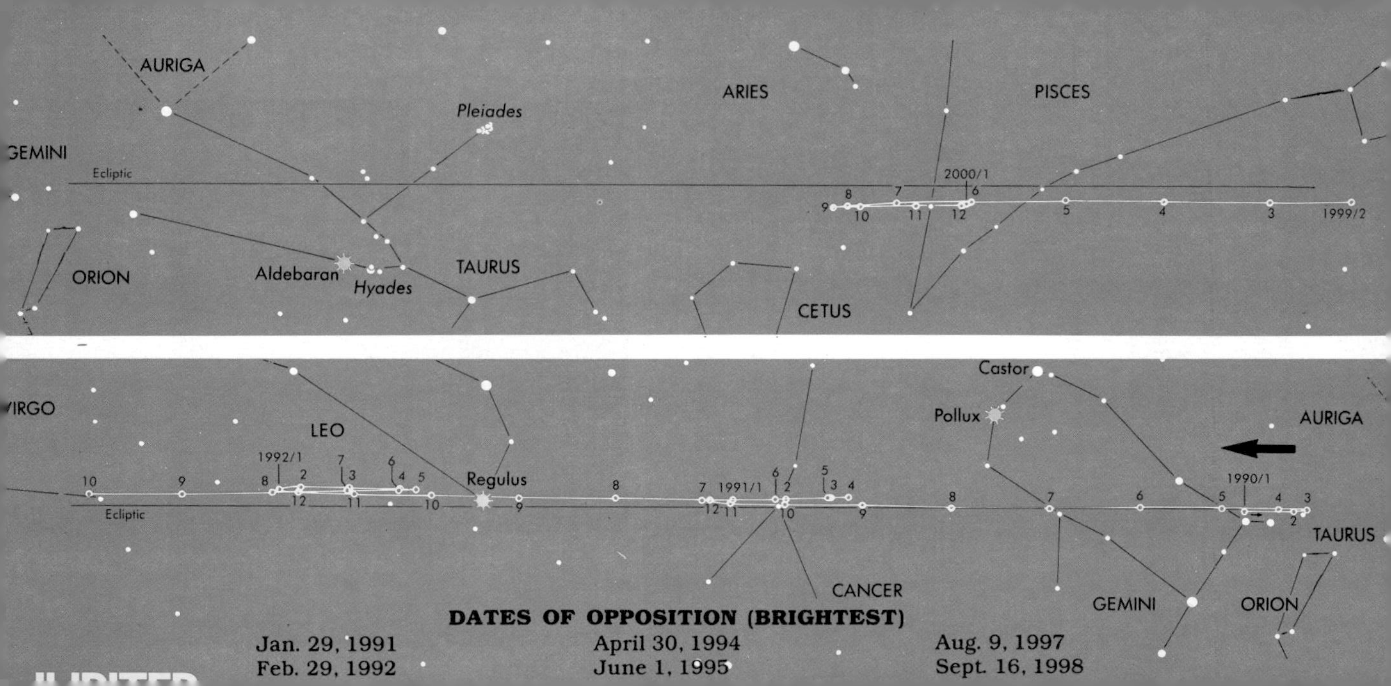
AURIGA
Pleiades
ARIES
PISCES
GEMINI
Ecliptic
2000/1
1999/2
ORION
Aldebaran
Hyades
TAURUS
CETUS
VIRGO
LEO
1992/1
Regulus
1991/1
CANCER
Castor
Pollux
AURIGA
1990/1
TAURUS
GEMINI
ORION
Ecliptic
DATES OF OPPOSITION (BRIGHTEST)
Jan. 29, 1991
Feb. 29, 1992
April 30, 1994
June 1, 1995
Aug. 9, 1997
Sept. 16, 1998

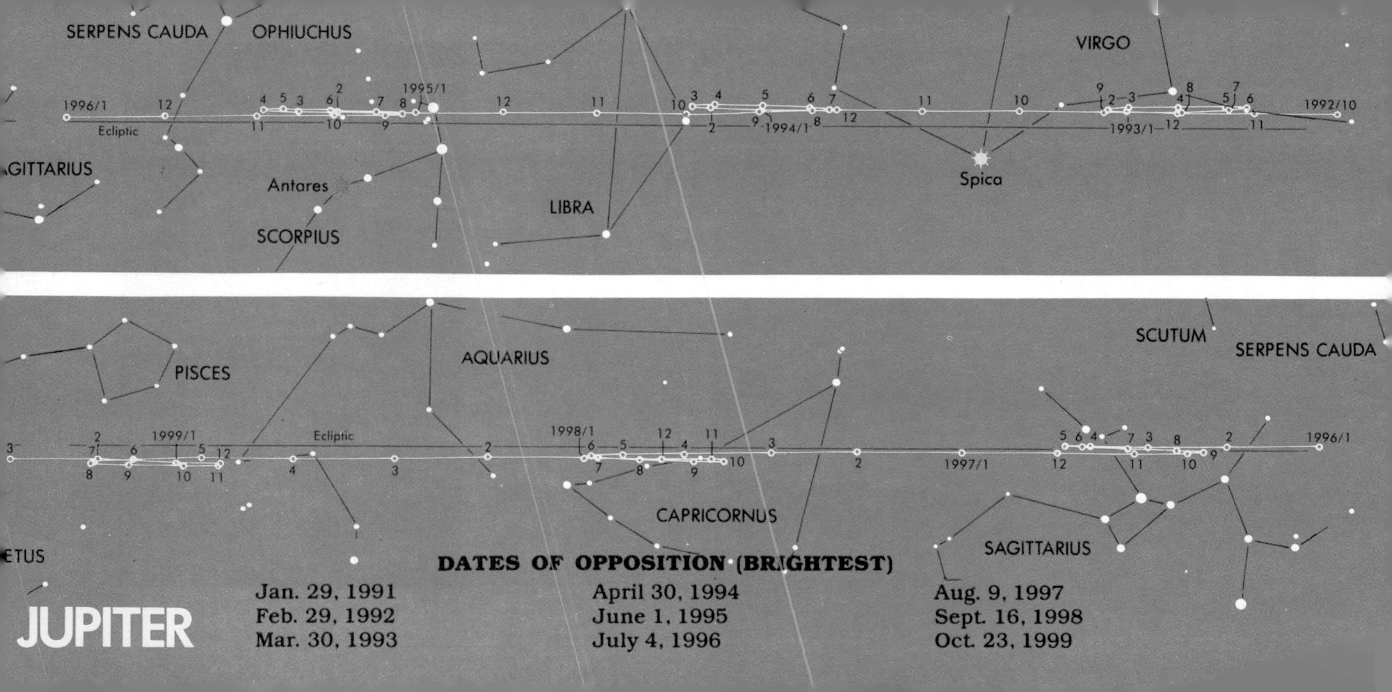

DATES OF OPPOSITION (BRIGHTEST)

Jan. 29, 1991	April 30, 1994	Aug. 9, 1997
Feb. 29, 1992	June 1, 1995	Sept. 16, 1998
Mar. 30, 1993	July 4, 1996	Oct. 23, 1999

Saturn

Saturn is the most glorious object to look at in the sky because of its magnificent rings. Even in a small telescope, their shape makes Saturn interesting to behold.

Saturn is so far from the Earth and sun — about ten times the distance from the sun to the Earth — that it does not change much in brightness over the year. It is roughly as bright as Betelgeuse. (Betelgeuse is the star that marks the shoulder of the constellation Orion, the Hunter, and is the tenth brightest star in the sky.)

Because Saturn's orbit is outside Earth's, it can be high in the sky at any hour of the day or night. Its position against the background of fixed stars is shown in the maps on pp. 78–79. The dates when Saturn is at opposition—highest at midnight and visible all night long —are given on the maps.

Saturn is a large planet, almost ten times the diameter of the Earth. Its ring is huge — about 20 Earth diameters across. As Saturn revolves around the sun, which takes about 30 Earth years, we see its rings at different angles. They are tilted 27° from Saturn's orbit. In the years before and after the rings are edge-on in 1995, we will be able to see one side or the other of the rings.

One of Saturn's moons, Titan (see p. 75), is bright enough to be seen with a small telescope or binoculars.

Saturn, photographed with a large telescope on Earth.

Saturn from the Voyagers

The Voyager spacecraft reached Saturn in 1980 and 1981, respectively. They revealed structure in Saturn's rings and showed us what many of Saturn's moons are like. They also measured Saturn's magnetic field, which is weaker at Saturn's surface than the magnetic field at the Earth's surface.

Seventeen moons are known to orbit Saturn. Three of the moons were found from the Voyager spacecraft. Saturn's largest moon is Titan, which at 3,200 miles (5,150 km) in diameter is larger than the planet Mercury. Among the moons in our solar system, only Jupiter's moon Ganymede is larger. In contrast to Jupiter's four large moons, which are roughly the same size, the rest of Saturn's moons are all much smaller. All of these moons are beyond Saturn's rings.

A phrase that can help you remember the names of Saturn's larger moons (more than 125 miles or 200 km in diameter) is: MET DR. THIP, which stands for Mimas, Enceladus, Tethys, Dione, Rhea, Titan, Hyperion, Iapetus, and Phoebe. Phoebe is much farther out than the other moons, and may be an asteroid captured by Saturn's gravity.

A montage showing Saturn and its larger moons, as photographed from the Voyager spacecraft. Clockwise from Titan, at upper right, we have Iapetus, at right center, and Tethys, at lower right; Mimas, in front of Saturn's disk; Dione, the large moon at lower left; Enceladus, at the end of Saturn's ring; and Rhea.

Saturn's Rings

As the Voyagers got closer and closer to Saturn, more and more detail was revealed in the rings. Ground-based photos had shown six major rings. From the Voyagers, we realized that there were a hundred ringlets (see below) dividing up these major rings. Astronomers were able to study the rings in finer detail when Voyager viewed the rings going in front of a star, and when the rings went in front of a star as seen from Earth in 1989. Hundreds of thousands of ringlets then appeared.

The rings are made of individual boulders, each the size of a car or smaller and each in an individual orbit around Saturn.

The dark division between Saturn's major rings, known as the Cassini Division, was long thought to be empty of material. Voyager revealed that some material actually orbits in this space. It shows in the photograph below as part of a ring in the midst of the blue-coded region. It would have been disastrous if one of the Voyager spacecraft had been sent through this region, as had been considered.

This view of Saturn's rings uses false colors to exaggerate slight differences in the color of the ringlets. Many of the narrow ringlets are visible. A photograph of the Earth, taken from space, is included for scale.

Planets have rings for the same reason that the Earth has tides — tidal forces.

Consider any two small objects that might otherwise attract each other by their own gravity and eventually form a moon. For any two objects at different distances from Saturn, the nearer one is pulled toward Saturn with a stronger force than the farther one. For any objects close enough to Saturn, this difference in Saturn's gravity is so great that the two objects remain separate and do not form a moon. Thus within a certain distance of each planet, objects orbiting around the planet form rings rather than moons.

Tides on Earth form in a similar manner. On the side of Earth closest to the moon at any given time, the moon's gravity pulls the water in the oceans toward the moon, harder than it pulls on the solid Earth. Since the whole solid Earth is pulled, on average, by the force of the moon's gravity at its middle, the water nearest the moon is pulled away from the Earth. On the other side of our planet, away from the moon, the Earth is pulled away from the water in the oceans, making a high tide there.

Saturn and its moons Tethys *(above)* and Dione, photographed by Voyager 1. The shadows of Saturn's rings and of Tethys can be seen on Saturn's cloud tops. Saturn's edge shows through the 2,200-mile- (3,500-km-) wide Cassini Division, an apparent gap between the rings.

Saturn's Mimas

Beyond Saturn's rings are five irregularly shaped moons. Four were discovered from spacecraft and one was discovered in recent years from Earth. The largest moon, Titan (see p. 75) is 140 miles × 120 miles × 100 miles (220 km × 200 km × 160 km) in size.

Next comes Mimas, Saturn's innermost major moon. Though it is only 240 miles (390 km) in diameter, it bears a huge crater, 80 miles (130 km) in diameter. The crater is named Herschel, after William Herschel, who discovered Uranus.

The crater Herschel is typical of the impact craters we find on our own moon and on other planets in having not only a raised rim but also a central peak. When a body such as a meteorite hits the surface of a moon or planet, the impact gives out so much energy that the result is as though an explosion has taken place. A round crater forms, even if the body has hit on a slant. The crater Herschel is so large compared with Mimas that its formation must have nearly broken Mimas apart.

Halfway around Mimas from Herschel is a large canyon. The canyon may have cracked open when the body that formed the huge crater hit the other side of Mimas. The rest of Mimas's surface is heavily cratered.

Saturn's moon Mimas, with its giant crater Herschel.

Saturn's Enceladus and Tethys

Enceladus is 320 miles (510 km) in diameter, half again bigger than Mimas. It has both smooth regions and craters. Grooves may be geologic faults, like those on Jupiter's moon Ganymede.

Saturn has four moons in the next size class, including Tethys, which is 660 miles (1,060 km) in diameter. Tethys has a giant crater named Odysseus (from the Greek myth) that is even larger than Herschel, the huge crater on Mimas. (Odysseus, though, does not cover as much of Tethys's surface.) Odysseus looks very flat. Its edges probably sagged as the ice surface of the crater melted and flowed. Thus Odysseus may have formed when Tethys was still warm inside, heated by energy left over from its formation.

Two other features on Tethys are the long canyon Ithaca and the crater Telemachus. Ithaca Chasma goes more than halfway around Tethys and is several miles deep.

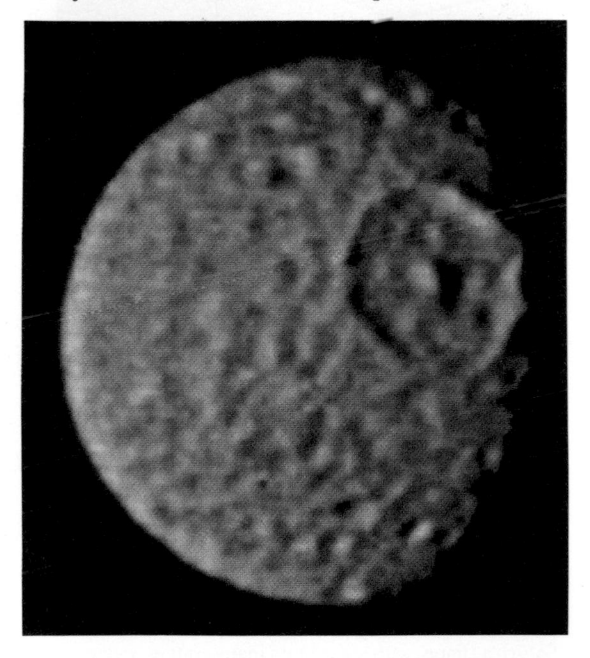

Saturn's moon Tethys, with its giant crater Odysseus.

Saturn's Dione and Rhea

Dione is 700 miles (1,120 km) in diameter. Like most of Saturn's moons, its surface is so cold that its ice is rigid, like rock. The density of this moon is almost the same as that of water, so much of the moon must be made of ice (frozen water).

A raised feature near Dione's top is Palatine Chasma. At upper left on its surface we see the crater Dido, with the crater Aeneas near the bottom. The pair of craters below Dido are named Remus (upper right) and Romulus, after the twin sons of the war god Mars who were the legendary founders of Rome.

The moon Rhea, 950 miles (1,530 km) in diameter, is named after the mother of Romulus and Remus. This moon also has parts that are heavily cratered and parts that show few craters. The lighter material on its surface may be ice (frozen water).

Saturn's Dione, with some of its many craters, valleys, and geologic faults.

Saturn's Titan

Titan, with a diameter of 3,200 miles (5,150 km), is larger than Mercury and is almost the size of Jupiter's moon Ganymede. Titan looks reddish even from afar.

The Voyagers found that Titan is covered with a thick atmosphere even denser than Earth's. The pressure at Titan's surface is higher than the atmospheric pressure at the Earth's surface (sea level). Like Earth's atmosphere, Titan's atmosphere is mostly nitrogen gas. It also contains some methane. The red color results from photochemical smog, a fate we hope doesn't happen to Earth's atmosphere.

Though the Voyagers were unable to look through Titan's smoggy atmosphere, they did detect layers of haze. Scientists learned the most about Titan's atmosphere when they studied how the radio signals from the Voyagers faded when the spacecraft went behind Titan.

Titan's surface is very cold, only −180°C (−290°F). Just as we find water in solid, liquid, and gaseous forms on Earth, methane may exist in all those forms on Titan. Titan may have methane lakes or oceans as well as methane ice and snow on its surface.

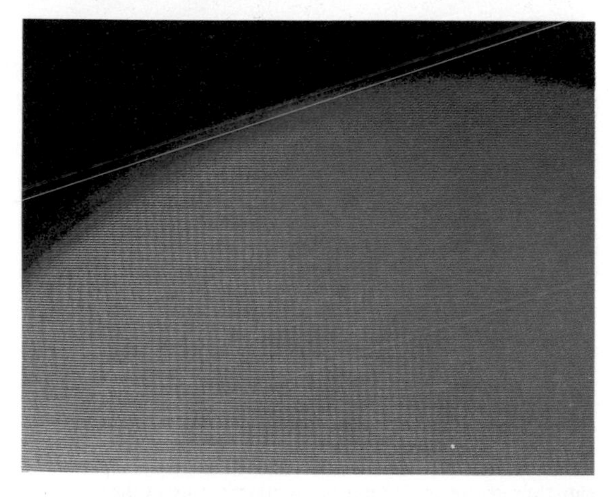

Titan's thick layers of smog.

Saturn's Hyperion and Iapetus

Beyond Titan is Hyperion, a flattened, hockey-puck or hamburger-shaped moon that is like a disk 250 miles (410 km) in diameter × 140 miles (220 km) thick.

Though Hyperion is the same size as Mimas, it looks very different. Its rotation does not seem to be stable. Apparently, small differences in the tug of gravity from neighboring moons sometimes change the direction of Hyperion's rotation. Its surface shows many craters, and perhaps some of the impacts also change its rotation.

Saturn's next moon (heading outward from the planet) is Iapetus, 910 miles (1,460 km) in diameter. Nobody understands just why one side of Iapetus is five times darker than the other side. The dark side is apparently coated with a dark material that may be similar to the dark material found on Halley's Comet and on some asteroids. Along with Tethys, Dione, and Titan, Iapetus was discovered more than 300 years ago. Mimas and Enceladus have been known to astronomers for over 200 years.

Saturn's outermost moon, Phoebe, may be a captured asteroid.

Saturn's Iapetus, a moon that is five times darker on one side than the other. The large circular feature at the edge of the dark side is Cassini Regio.

Departing Saturn

As the Voyager spacecraft left Saturn, they got a few views of the planet in its crescent phase, views that could never be seen from Earth. Saturn's dark shadow shows clearly on the rings, but the rings are nevertheless transparent enough that Saturn's disk shows through.

Among the strangest features seen on Saturn were the "spokes," features in the rings that go in and out instead of around the planet. Scientists had expected that, because of gravity's role in making the rings, all features in them would arrange themselves along the rings rather than across them. The spokes are dark as seen from the spacecraft approaching from the Earth's direction (see p. 69) and bright when looking back. This information tells us that they are made of small bits of dust. Perhaps the dust is held above Saturn's rings by electrical charge.

The maps on the next two pages show where Saturn can be seen in the sky against the background of fixed stars. Compare these positions with the monthly star charts in the *Peterson First Guide to Astronomy.*

Saturn, seen from Voyager 1 as it departed.

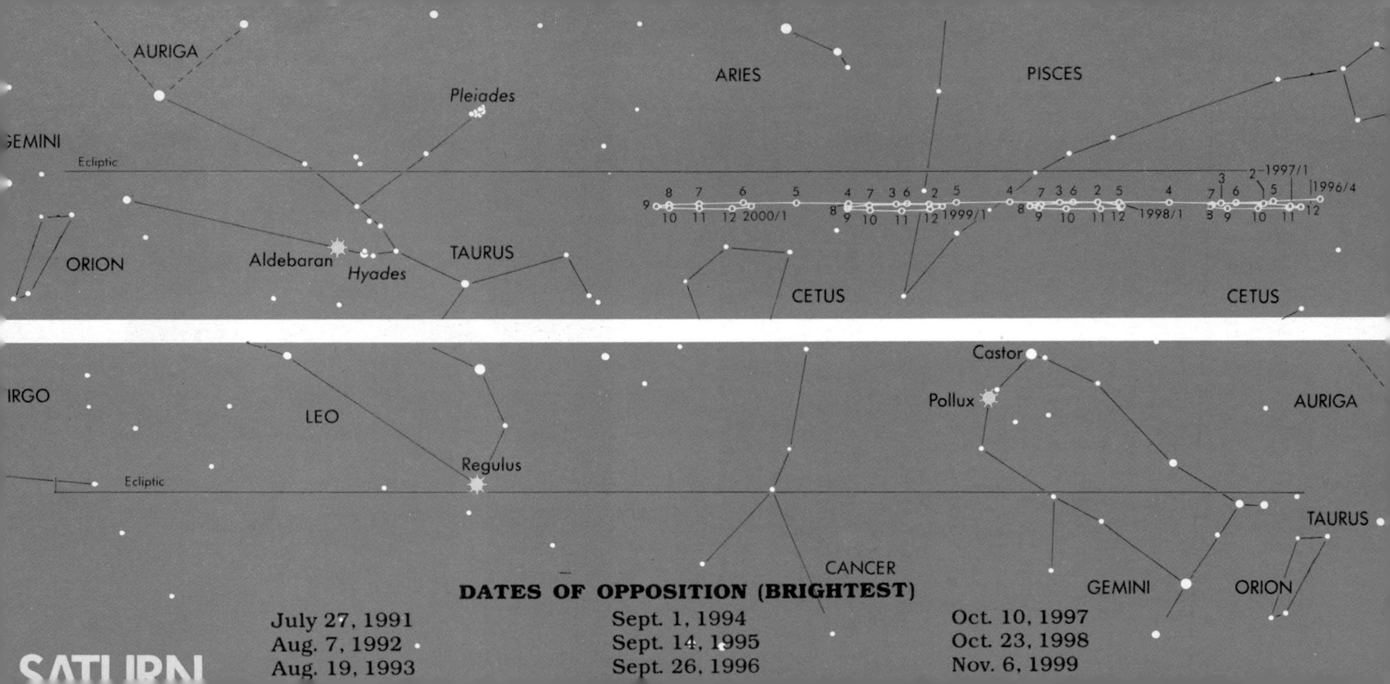

DATES OF OPPOSITION (BRIGHTEST)

July 27, 1991	Sept. 1, 1994	Oct. 10, 1997
Aug. 7, 1992	Sept. 14, 1995	Oct. 23, 1998
Aug. 19, 1993	Sept. 26, 1996	Nov. 6, 1999

Uranus

Uranus, the seventh planet from the sun, is 32,400 miles (52,142 km) in diameter, four times the diameter of our Earth. Uranus and Neptune are similar in size, somewhat smaller than Jupiter and Saturn, and each contains about fifteen times the mass of the Earth. Uranus was the first planet discovered in modern times; it was not known to the ancients. It was found in 1781 by William Herschel.

Uranus orbits about twice as far out from the sun as Saturn. It is never close enough to Earth for us to see detail on its surface with ground-based telescopes. Uranus takes 84 of our years to orbit the sun.

Most unusually, Uranus rotates on its side. Its equator makes almost a right angle with the plane of its orbit around the sun. Thus the north pole of Uranus points toward the sun for 42 years and is then in darkness for 42 years, while the south pole of Uranus is in sight of the sun. Studying this strange heating pattern may give us insights into Earth's weather. Uranus is just too faint to be seen with the naked eye, and shows only as a point of light in any telescope.

A montage of images of Uranus and its moons, from Voyager 2. In front of Uranus (the blue-green image) is Ariel, and Miranda is just above Uranus. Titania is at top, Oberon is at Uranus's right, and Umbriel is at bottom.

Uranus from Voyager

Saturn's gravitational pull bent the path of the Voyager 1 spacecraft so it would head up out of the plane of our solar system and into interstellar space. The path of the Voyager 2 spacecraft, on the other hand, was bent toward Uranus. It reached Uranus in 1986. Circled by moons orbiting perpendicularly to its orbit, Uranus and its system were like a bull's eye for the spacecraft and its cameras.

Uranus itself shows very little structure on its surface. It appears blue-green because the methane gas in its atmosphere absorbs all the other colors in the sunlight that hits it. The methane is an impurity in the hydrogen gas that makes up most of Uranus's atmosphere.

Only three small clouds have been detected on Uranus. By following these clouds, astronomers were able to figure out that it takes 16 to 17 hours for Uranus to rotate on its axis, depending on latitude. Voyager 2 also detected bursts of radio waves given off by Uranus. The bursts repeat every 17.24 hours, so astronomers concluded that this must be the rotation period of Uranus's interior.

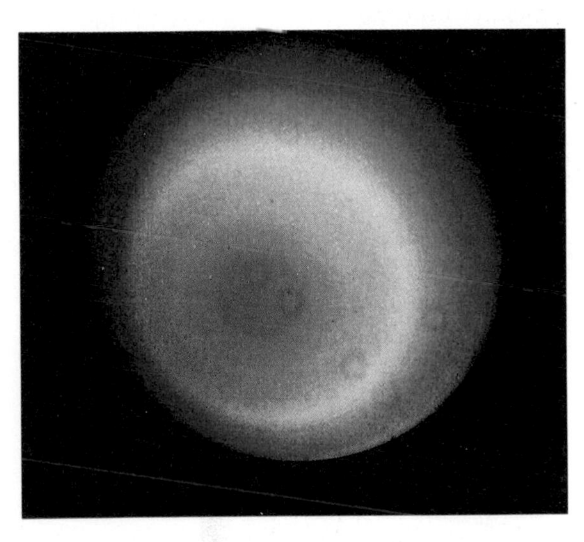

A false-color composite image of Uranus. The doughnut shapes are out-of-focus dust in the camera.

Uranus's Rings

A major discovery about Uranus was made not from spacecraft but from telescopes on or near the Earth. In 1977, Uranus passed in front of a distant star. Scientists observed this event from an airplane equipped with a telescope. About half an hour before Uranus was to begin covering the star, the star began winking on and off a few times, as though something were covering it. After Uranus's disk (the planet itself) seemed to have passed the star, the star again winked on and off. Telescopes on the ground also picked up many of these changes in brightness. Scientists realized that Uranus had nine rings that, in turn, blocked the starlight from reaching us.

Each of Uranus's rings is narrow, only a few miles across. The widest is the outermost ring, which ranges from 13 miles (20 km) to 60 miles (100 km) across and is not quite round.

When the Voyagers flew by Uranus, they detected not only the nine rings previously known but also two more rings that were even fainter. The images transmitted by the Voyager spacecraft also revealed two small moons, Cordelia and Ophelia, whose gravity seems to shepherd the material for the outer ring.

A Voyager photograph showing the nine rings of Uranus that had been discovered from Earth.

Uranus's Moons

Astronomers on Earth had known that Uranus had five moons: Miranda, Ariel, Umbriel, Titania, and Oberon. The Voyager spacecraft discovered ten additional small moons, all inside the orbit of Miranda. The names of all Uranus's moons come from plays of Shakespeare and a poem by Alexander Pope.

Ariel, Umbriel, Titania, and Oberon are roughly the size of the middle-sized moons of Saturn. Ariel and Umbriel are 720 to 740 miles (1,160 to 1,190 km) in diameter. Titania and Oberon are 1,000 and 960 miles (1,610 and 1,550 km) in diameter, respectively. They are only 50% denser than water, which shows that ices of some type are present. The ices could be frozen water, ammonia, methane, and other compounds. All these moons are gray in color and fairly dark. Perhaps they are covered with carbon, which could be soot or graphite.

Ariel shows a crust with fractures and geologic faults. It has few large craters. Material apparently flowed from underneath its surface. This moon has been geologically active.

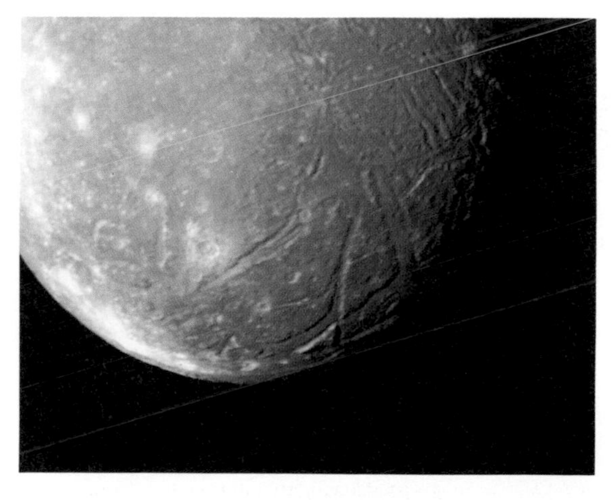

Uranus's moon Ariel, with craters and valleys.

Uranus's Moons

Umbriel, about the same size as Ariel, is darker. Of Uranus's moons, it shows the least geological activity. It is covered with so many craters that its surface must not have been changed for billions of years, except when the impact of meteorites formed new craters. So we may be seeing a surface that dates back to the formation of our solar system, 4.5 billion years ago. One bright ring on Umbriel may be a frost-covered crater.

Titania and Oberon are twice as far out as Ariel and Umbriel and somewhat larger. Titania has many small craters but few large ones. The larger craters that should have been there at one time must have been covered by material that flowed out of Titania's interior. The Voyagers detected many geologic faults and lines of cliffs on Titania.

Oberon, by contrast, has many large craters more than 60 miles (100 km) across. Some dark patches on the floors of craters may be of the same material that darkens one side of Saturn's moon Iapetus. This dark material apparently flowed from inside Oberon. A mountain more than 12 miles (20 km) high was photographed by the Voyagers.

Miranda, Uranus's outermost moon, is one of the strangest objects in the solar system (see p. 85).

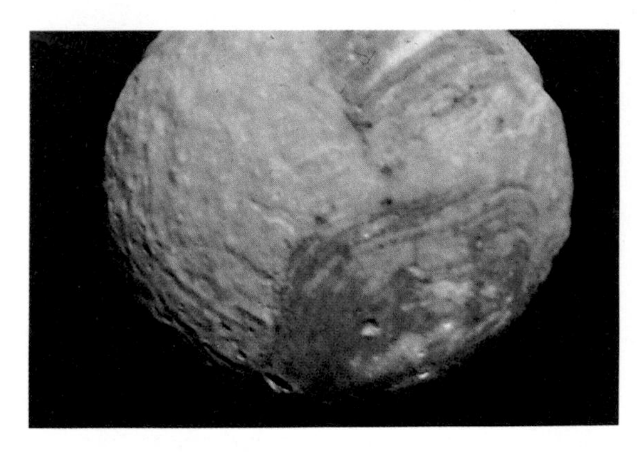

Uranus's moon Miranda.

Uranus's Miranda

Miranda's surface contains extraordin contrasts and different types of regions. E though Miranda is only 300 miles (484 km) diameter, it is more varied than other bodies in the solar system.

Parts of Miranda are covered with plains and parts have parallel dark bands. One set of bands even has sharp corners. Scientists think that these unusual features formed after a collision long ago broke Miranda apart. When gravity brought the pieces together again, the pieces were jumbled (see p. 84).

Perhaps the most remarkable feature on Miranda is a giant canyon a few miles deep.

The ten additional moons discovered by the Voyagers are all very dark, reflecting less than half as much sunlight as the other moons of Uranus. The largest of these moons, Puck, is 105 miles (170 km) in diameter and is closest to Miranda. Puck was named after the mischievous sprite in Shakespeare's *Midsummer Night's Dream.*

A montage of Voyager photographs of Miranda's canyon, with Uranus in the background. Uranus's ring has been drawn on.

Neptune

[illegible]une orbits the sun at an average distance [illegible] again farther than Uranus, 30 times the [illegible]stance between the Earth and the sun. Nep[illegible]une is so far away that from Earth we can see little detail on its surface. Nonetheless, we have been able to tell from changes in its clouds that this planet shows more activity than Uranus. In 1989, Voyager 2 flew by Neptune and astronomers were able to study the planet and its moons closely for the first time.

Neptune, like Uranus, looks like a small, blue-green disk in the sky. It moves slowly among the stars, completing an orbit around the sun only once every 165 years. So Neptune has not even completed a single orbit since it was discovered in 1846.

The position of Neptune was predicted before its actual discovery, from mathematical studies of the orbit of Uranus. The gravity of Neptune exerted a pull on Uranus, causing Uranus's orbit to be not quite elliptical.

Neptune with its Great Dark Spot, as seen from Voyager 2.

Neptune and Its Moons

Voyager 2 revealed a Great Dark Spot o
tune, a spiral storm the size of Earth. Ur
on the other hand, shows little atmospher
structure. The difference no doubt comes fr
the fact that Neptune has an internal heat source that gives the planet about as much energy as it gets from the sun. Uranus, on the other hand, gives off almost precisely as much energy as it receives from the sun. Neptune's atmosphere, also, is not subject to the same unusual heating pattern as Uranus's.

Two moons of Neptune were known from Earth-based studies. The larger moon, Triton, was named after a son of Poseidon, a sea god like Neptune in Greek mythology. Studies from Earth showed that Triton has methane on it or in its atmosphere.

The smaller of Neptune's known moons, Nereid, was named from the Greek word for sea nymph. Its orbit is very out of round and is fifteen times larger than Triton's. Voyager 2 discovered six more moons, including one larger than Nereid.

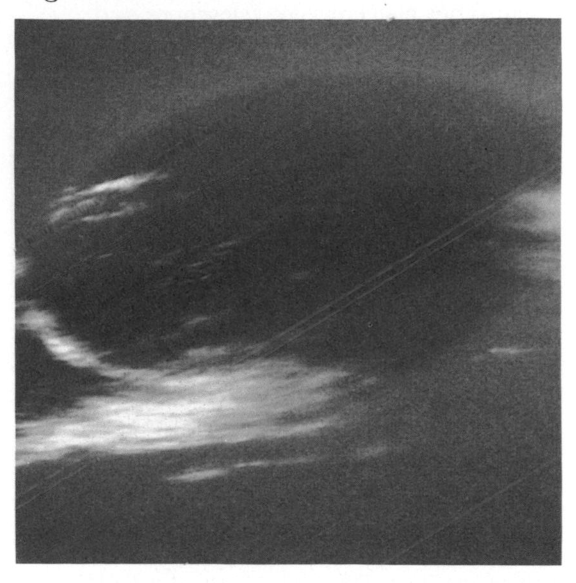

A close-up view of Neptune's Great Dark Spot and its high-altitude clouds.

r at Neptune

2 reached Neptune on August 24–25, Its path near Jupiter, Saturn, and Ura- had been set by the need to go on to the t planet in the series. The spacecraft was ot intended to study any other planets after Neptune, so it was able to fly by Triton at extremely close range (see p. 89). Voyager 2 also went by in a path from which it could view Triton blocking the sun. From the way in which the sun's light dimmed, the spacecraft could measure Triton's atmosphere.

As Voyager 2 approached Triton, the moon seemed to shrink. Instead of being as large as Jupiter's Ganymede or Saturn's Titan, Triton turned out to be roughly half that size, smaller than Earth's moon.

The Voyager spacecraft was 12 years old when it reached Neptune, and some of its equipment had failed. Also, it was so much farther from the Earth than it had been when it flew by the other planets that its radio signal was weaker. Engineers on Earth designed new ways to receive the signals and to strengthen them. They also enlarged telescopes and brought new large telescopes into play to receive the signals from Voyager 2 on the crucial day.

Neptune and Triton. Triton reflects so much of the light that hits it that it fooled astronomers into thinking it was larger than it is.

Voyager and Triton

Images of Neptune and its moons were taken by Voyager 2 through a set of different color filters. The individual black-and-white images could be printed in sets to make color pictures. The blue-green color of Neptune, caused by methane in its atmosphere, was apparent. The spacecraft had to go closer to make the best studies of the hydrogen and helium that make up most of Neptune's atmosphere.

Triton's atmosphere turned out to be mostly nitrogen, like Earth's. But Triton is much, much colder—this distant moon is evidently the coldest place in our solar system.

Triton's surface is strange and jumbled. It has cliffs, faults, and a few craters. Materials on the moon's surface may have warmed and refrozen many times. Voyager photos of the surface revealed the effects of ice vulcanism, in which mushy ice flowed slowly through cracks in Triton's crust, onto its surface. Some of the ice, which is frozen methane, not water, turned pinkish as it was hit by radiation from the sun.

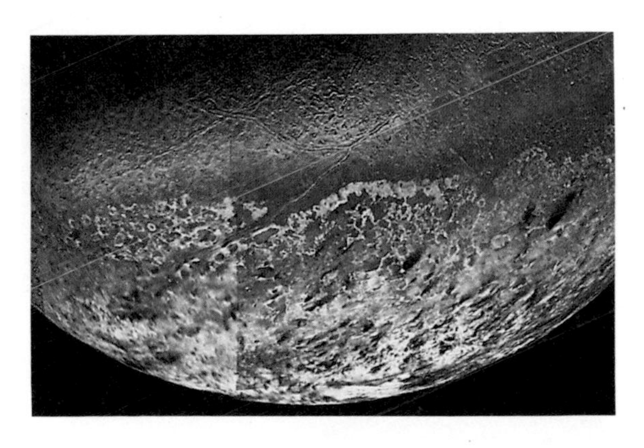

A combination of pictures of Triton. At bottom is its south polar cap, with dark streaks of material that may have erupted. At upper left is the "cantaloupe" terrain.

Voyager at Neptune

The major part of Voyager 2's passage through the Neptune system was to search for rings. Ever since rings were discovered around Uranus, scientists had searched for rings around Neptune by the same process. Over the years, they watched closely on several occasions when Neptune passed in front of stars. Surprisingly, sometimes the star winked out before and after Neptune passed in front of it and sometimes not. Many of these winkings were picked up by several telescopes, so astronomers believed that they were real events. Further, once one telescope saw a winking and another telescope nearby did not. The best explanation seemed to be that Neptune had rings but that the rings did not fill the whole path around the planet.

The Voyager images showed that Neptune has several rings. The rings do go all the way around the planet, but are clumpy. Material in the inner ring extends down to Neptune's cloudtops.

Some astronomers worked on theories that explained how ring material could be kept in only part of the ring path. These theories are based on the idea that, like the narrow ringlets of Saturn and the narrow rings of Uranus, Neptune's ring arcs are held in position by the gravity from small moons orbiting the planet.

Neptune has several rings that go all around it, though one obviously has clumps of material in it.

Beyond Neptune

Voyager 2 went by Neptune and then, for seven hours, it went very close to Triton. Later, it studied Nereid, but not from as close up. It also searched for a magnetic field around Neptune and studied particles in interplanetary space.

From Neptune, Voyager 2 is continuing out into space. It is still in the region where the particles flowing outward from the sun — the "*solar wind*" — are still very important. In a few decades, Voyager 2 may reach the edge of our solar system, where the sun's particles are no longer so important.

Voyager 2 has transmitted an impressive set of images and information over a 12-year period, coming close to Jupiter, Saturn, Uranus, and Neptune, and several dozen of their moons.

The view looking back from beyond Neptune and Triton.

Pluto

Pluto is an odd planet in several ways. It is a small planet with a solid surface, located just past large gaseous planets. Its orbit is much more out of round than any other planet's and is much more tilted. Pluto also has a moon almost its own size.

Pluto was named after the Greek god of the underworld. This planet wasn't discovered until 1930. Even after Neptune had been discovered, some uncertainties remained about the reasons why Uranus's orbit wasn't a perfect ellipse. Astronomers predicted that a planet at the position of Pluto could explain the problem. A careful search of the sky turned up Pluto, though we now know that it doesn't have enough mass to distort Uranus's orbit with the pull of its gravity.

Photos of Pluto were taken through large telescopes from time to time. In 1978, a scientist noticed that one of the pictures taken to study Pluto's orbit looked strange. Pluto's image wasn't quite round. The scientist realized that he was seeing a glimpse of a moon traveling around Pluto. He named the moon Charon, after both the mythological oarsman who rowed people across the river to the underworld, and his wife.

Pluto and its moon Charon.

Pluto and Charon

It is very valuable to be able to study a moon around a planet. The period (time) the moon takes to make its orbit depends on its distance from the planet and on its mass. Even though scientists could not measure the distance from Pluto to Charon very accurately, they still knew enough to improve their knowledge of Pluto's mass. Pluto turned out to have only about 1/500 the mass of the Earth, much less than astronomers had thought. Pluto has far too little mass to have affected the orbit of Uranus noticeably.

In 1983, an international spacecraft named IRAS, the Infrared Astronomical Satellite, studied Pluto. Scientists studying the observations concluded that Pluto's surface is not uniform. Pluto probably has a dark band around its equator. It also probably has caps of frozen methane around its poles. The polar caps should vary over one of Pluto's years, which are about 250 Earth years long.

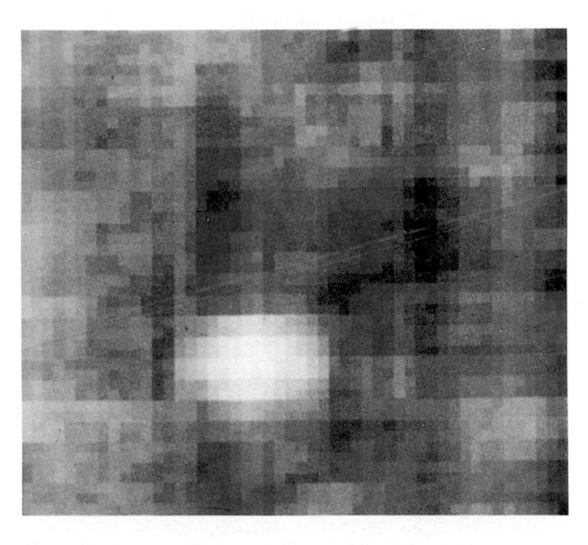

The yellow spot is Pluto and Charon blurred together, in a false-color image made from the Infrared Astronomical Satellite. The colors were originally picked up by a sensitive infrared scanner on the satellite and were converted into these colors by computer. The rest of the frame shows fainter background sources of infrared light.

Pluto and Charon

We are lucky to be observing Pluto at the current part of its 250-year-long orbit. The distant planet reached the near point to the sun in its orbit in 1989. At that point Pluto became about as bright as it ever gets, as seen from Earth. Also, only twice in Pluto's orbit around the sun is Charon's orbit around Pluto aligned so that the moon goes between Pluto and the Earth. Charon orbits Pluto in the same time that Pluto takes to rotate on its axis, 6.4 days. Thus if we were on Pluto, Charon would always seem to be in the same spot in the sky.

Every 6.4 days between 1985 and 1989, Charon went in front of Pluto. In between, Charon went behind Pluto. In either case, the total amount of light from Charon and Pluto together dropped. So even without being able to tell Charon and Pluto apart from our distance, astronomers could study how big they are, how far they are away from each other, and what their surfaces are like.

The way that Pluto and Charon hide each other has told us that Pluto is 1,430 miles (2,285 km) in diameter and Charon is 745 miles (1,200 km) in diameter. Thus Charon is 53% the diameter of Pluto, which makes it the largest moon in the solar system when com-

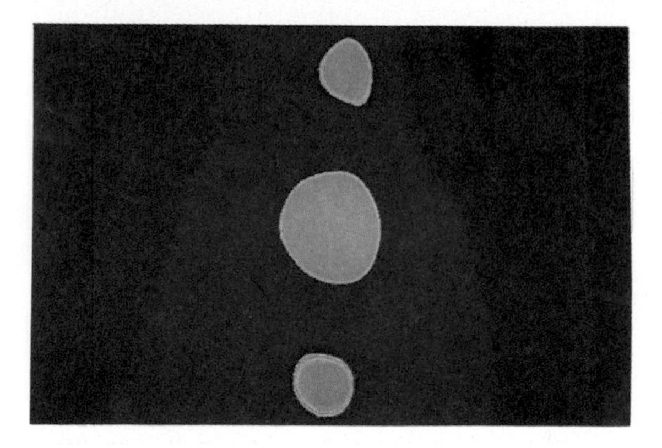

A special technique uses many very short exposures to overcome the blurring of the Earth's atmosphere. The results of this "speckle" method show the correct separation of Pluto *(middle)* and Charon, but we don't know whether the top image or the bottom one is Charon.

pared to the size of its parent planet. Pluto is less than half the size of the planet Mercury and is only ⅔ the size of our moon.

When Charon is completely behind Pluto, all the light we receive comes from Pluto alone. Astronomers study the colors in Pluto's light to see which gases and other materials are present on the planet. Each material has its own set of colors. Then they can subtract Pluto's light from the total light of Pluto and Charon together. The result shows Charon's set of colors alone. Study of this set of colors has shown that the ices on Charon are mostly frozen water rather than methane or ammonia frost. The hiding of Charon has also shown that Pluto reflects 50% of the sunlight that hits it. Charon, in contrast, is darker. It reflects only 37% of the sunlight that hits it. Studies of the details of the amount of light even allow astronomers to figure out the extent to which different parts of Pluto's and Charon's surfaces vary in lightness and darkness.

Pluto's density is so low that scientists have concluded that it must be made of ices. Pluto may be more similar to the moons of the outer planets than it is to the other major planets.

A model of the darkness patterns on Pluto and Charon that explains the changes in light received by telescopes when these two objects hide each other. Pluto has a dark band near its equator, and light polar caps.

Our Sun

The nine planets we have discussed orbit around the sun, the central object in our solar system. The sun is a star that shines with energy generated deep inside it. All of the light we get from the planets, on the other hand, is reflected sunlight.

The sun is 870,000 miles (1,400,000 km) across. A million Earths would fit inside it. The everyday surface of the sun that lights up our daytime sky is called the *photosphere*, meaning "the sphere the light comes from." It is too bright to stare at safely. Scientists and amateur astronomers either project an image of the sun onto a wall or screen or else use special filters that cut out all but about one-millionth of the sun's light.

Using proper precautions, one can see dark sunspots on the sun's surface. The presence of these sunspots has been known since they were seen by Galileo in 1610. Records of the sunspots from day to day show that the sun rotates on its axis about once every 25 days. Different latitudes rotate at slightly different speeds.

The sun, with sunspots on it.

The Solar Surface and Interior

It is difficult to study the inside of the sun, below the photosphere, because we cannot see it. But scientists have concluded that the extremely hot gases in the outer third of the sun are in convection, like boiling. Below that, energy is carried by radiation.

The center of the sun is at a temperature of 15,000,000°C (27,000,000°F). A high temperature like that means that particles there are moving very fast. The moving particles are nuclei of atoms, since it is so hot at the sun's center that the electrons that surround the nuclei are stripped off. The hydrogen nuclei are moving so fast that they can fuse with each other, even though their positive charges try to push them apart. The result is that hydrogen nuclei fuse, one at a time, to make helium. The resulting helium contains slightly less mass than the four hydrogen nuclei that went into it. The difference has been changed into a large amount of energy. When the energy reaches the sun's surface, we see it as light.

We would like to know how to duplicate this fusion process on Earth, to make energy here. Several research projects are devoted to this important task.

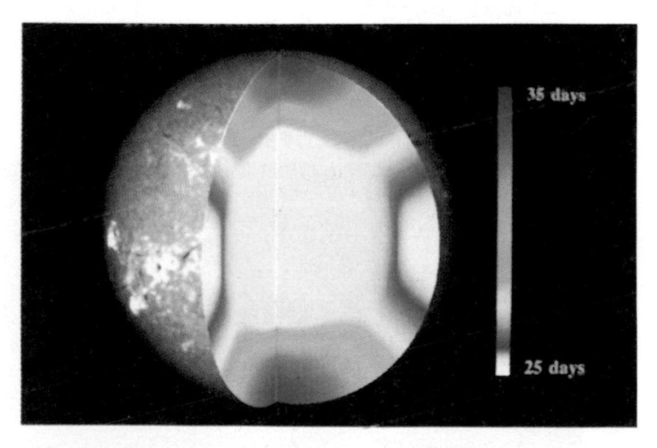

A cutaway view of the sun's interior, color-coded to show differences in the time it takes (25–35 days) for different parts of the sun to complete one full rotation. The rotation rates were found from measurements of the sun's surface as it "rings" (moves in and out — see p. 98). The surface shows how the sun looks through a filter that passes only light from hydrogen gas (see p. 102).

Studying the Sun

Though we cannot see the sun's interior directly, we can find out about it by studying its surface. Parts of the surface move in and out regularly, as shown on the previous page. The sun is ringing, like a bell in a sandstorm that is regularly struck by bits of sand. The periods — the repetition times — of the ringing reveal what the temperature and density of different layers inside are like. The sun's surface rotation persists ¼ of the way in; beyond that, the interior rotates rigidly with a 27-day period (see p. 97).

Astronomers also find out about the sun's center by searching for particles called neutrinos. Neutrinos should be given off whenever fusion (see p. 97) takes place. Scientists are doing research to discover why the number of neutrinos detected from the sun is smaller than had been expected.

The picture below shows a plot of sunspots. Each few months, a vertical strip is filled in with the latitude of the sunspots on the sun. The number of sunspots is shown with color. When the spots have been plotted for many years, we can see that sunspots first form at higher latitudes on the sun's surface and then form at lower ones. Every 11 years or so, the number of sunspots on the sun goes through a peak. This period is the sunspot cycle. The most recent peak was in 1990.

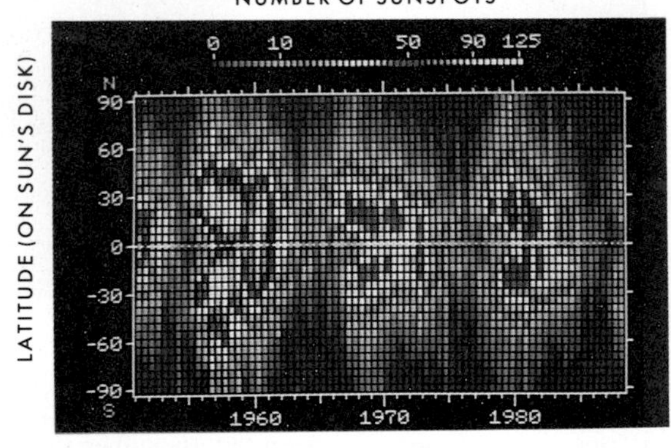

The "butterfly diagram" shows changes over time in the number of sunspots and their latitudes.

Solar Eclipses

Every month, the new moon comes when our moon is close to the sun in the sky and its back side is lighted. But the moon's orbit is tilted, so it usually misses covering the sun exactly. Two to four times a year, the moon covers a bit of the sun's surface, the photosphere. We have a *partial solar eclipse.* And about once every year and a half, the moon covers the photosphere precisely. This circumstance makes a *total solar eclipse.*

The sun is 400 times larger than the moon, and it is also 400 times farther away. So the sun and the moon seem to cover about the same amount of our sky. Because the moon's orbit around the Earth is not exactly round, sometimes the moon is larger in the sky— large enough to more than cover the sun by up to 10%, while sometimes it is slightly smaller than the sun. An eclipse that occurs when the moon doesn't quite cover the sun leaves a ring — an annulus — of sunlight, and is called an *annular eclipse.* An annular eclipse will cover much of the continental United States on May 10, 1994.

The solar corona surrounds the dark side of the moon during a total solar eclipse.

Solar Eclipses

The path of a total or annular eclipse is only a few miles or up to a few hundred miles wide. The path across the Earth's surface can be thousands of miles long. You must be standing in this narrow path to see the wonderful parts of a solar eclipse. Otherwise, whatever part of the photosphere is left gives off too much light. The partial phases of an eclipse are visible over a wider area.

Someone in the path of a total eclipse will see the moon gradually cover the sun for up to two hours. Special filters are necessary to view the sun safely during this phase. Next, as shown below, the moon covers all the sun's surface, or photosphere, except for a point of light that shines through a valley on the edge of the moon. The effect is that of a glimmering diamond ring.

When all the photosphere is covered, it becomes safe to view the eclipse without a special filter, but only for as long as the total part of the eclipse lasts. First, a pinkish rim, the chromosphere, is visible for a few seconds. Then the solar corona appears for a short time; the longest total eclipse lasts about 7 minutes.

The solar corona is a beautiful, pearly white outer layer of the sun. It contains gas that is 2,000,000°C (about 4,000,000°F). Streamers of corona are different at different parts of the sunspot cycle.

The diamond-ring effect during a total solar eclipse.

The Sun from Space

Most of the solar corona is best studied from the ground, during eclipses. Other parts of the solar corona can be studied well from satellites in space. An x-ray view, like the one on this page, shows the hot gas from the corona even over the center of the sun's disk. The photosphere behind the corona looks dark, because it does not give off x-rays.

One of the major questions of solar studies is why the corona is so hot. The x-ray picture shows that the corona is brightest and hottest in the solar-active regions. Below the corona, those active regions contain the sunspots. The sunspots are regions of very high magnetic field, thousands of times stronger than the average magnetic field of the Earth or sun. Thus it seems reasonable that the corona is heated by some means that involves magnetic fields.

Most of the studies of the sun are made from satellites with sensors that detect types of light that do not come through the Earth's atmosphere. The views of the sun with the finest detail still come from telescopes on Earth.

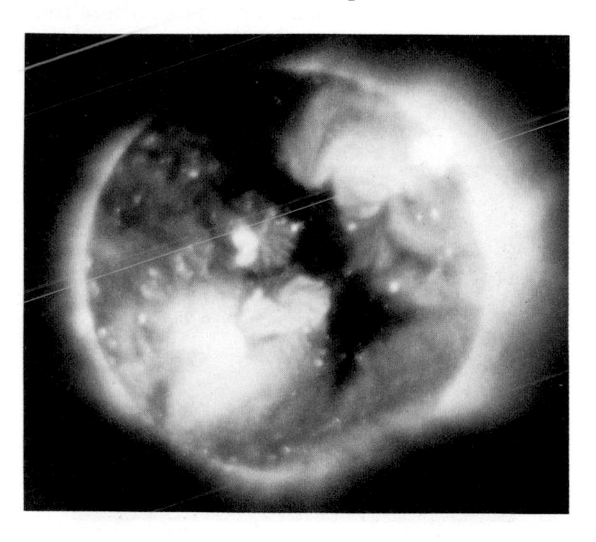

An x-ray view of the sun. The dark regions are known as "coronal holes." They are regions where the corona is cooler and less dense.

Observing the Sun

There are several ways to observe the sun from Earth on an everyday basis. Except during eclipses, a telescope is usually necessary, though a small telescope will do. The prime thing to remember is *never to look at the everyday surface of the sun directly*, without special filters.

One way to use a telescope is with "eyepiece projection," in which the eyepiece is put behind its normal focus. The solar image is then projected on a wall or screen. The image contains all the colors of sunlight, and is known as a white-light image. You can use eyepiece projection to study the sunspots and how they change from day to day. You can follow the sun's rotation. You can also see that the sun is darker near its edge than near its center. This darkening shows that the sun gets cooler as you go outward in the photosphere. Near the sun's edge, we get light from these cooler, darker layers.

A special filter for the sun that passes only the light of hydrogen gives images like the one below. On the sun's surface, we see dark filaments going across, near the region where the sunspots are in white light. At the sun's edge, we see what the filaments look like when we look at them sideways. Then they are silhouetted against the sky, and are called *prominences.*

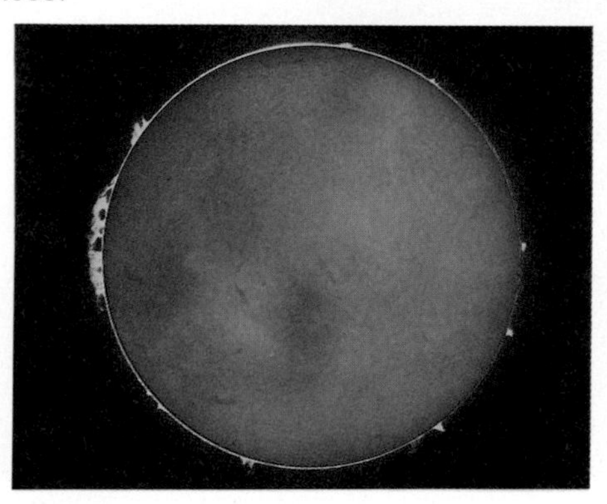

Two images taken with a hydrogen-light filter. The inner image of the sun's disk has been placed into an outer image with a longer exposure that shows prominences.

Solar Activity and the Earth

Solar prominences can be calm structures, and can last for weeks on the sun. They are about 15,000°C (27,000°F).

Solar flares — much more violent events — sometimes occur on the sun. These flares can reach much hotter temperatures and send particles and x-rays out into space, adding to the steady flow of particles called the *solar wind*. Sometimes the particles reach the Earth's atmosphere about three or four days later. They hit atoms in our atmosphere and make them glow. We see these glowing atoms as the aurora borealis, or northern lights (see below).

Flares and auroras occur more often at the peak of the sunspot cycle. Flares sometimes disrupt radio transmissions and satellite communications and cause power blackouts.

The aurora is but one sign of a link between the sun and the Earth. The sun not only warms the Earth each day but also surely affects the Earth's climate in the long term.

The aurora borealis, or northern lights, following the giant solar flare in March 1989.

Comets

Comets, it has been said, are the closest things to nothing that anything can be. Though they start as small chunks of ice and rock only about 10 miles (16 km) across, when they come close to the sun their tails can extend over millions of miles of space. They are the largest objects in the solar system.

Every ten years or so, a comet appears that is spectacular even to the naked eye. But in an average year, a dozen fainter comets may be discovered. Most can be viewed only through telescopes or binoculars.

A comet has two tails: a gas tail, which looks bluish, and a dust tail, which looks more yellowish. The appearance of these tails can change from hour to hour or day to day. If you hear that a bright comet will be in view, make sure to see it right away. It might be spectacular for only a day or two, and you might only have a day or a week of notice. Comet West, in 1976, met that description.

The bright base of the comet is its head. In the head is a small nucleus of solid material surrounded by a gaseous coma.

Comet West showed a bluish gas tail and a yellower dust tail.

Halley's Comet

In 1680 and 1682, the scientists Isaac Newton and Edmond Halley observed bright comets. In the following years, as a result of Halley's urging, Newton wrote his masterpiece that included the law of gravity.

In 1705, Halley applied Newton's law of gravity to observations of comets. He deduced that the bright comet that had been seen in 1682 was the same as the comets that had been seen in 1531 and 1607. He explained the slight difference in the period between the returns as an effect of Jupiter's gravity. He predicted that the comet would return in 1758.

When the comet indeed returned in 1758, it confirmed not only Halley's prediction but also Newton's law of gravity. The comet has been known ever since as "Halley's Comet."

Brighter comets than Halley's Comet appear occasionally, but Halley's Comet is the only reasonably bright comet that appears regularly. People know the tales of its previous appearances. Halley's Comet is a link with the world's history.

Because we know this comet's orbit so well, the comet was located while it was quite far out in the solar system, well before it came close to Earth again in 1986.

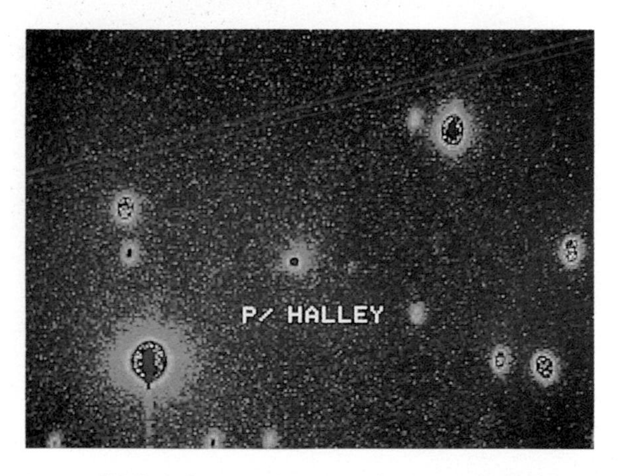

A view of Halley's Comet, taken more than two years before it came closest to the sun. No other comet has been detected that early.

Halley's Comet

Comets travel in very elongated orbits. The orbit of Halley's Comet takes it within the Earth's orbit and beyond the orbit of Neptune. When comets are far from the sun, only their icy and rocky nuclei are present. The theory is that comet nuclei are "dirty snowballs" — icy snowballs with some rocks and dust mixed in.

As a comet approaches the sun, the energy in sunlight turns some of the ice into gas. The coma forms. As the comet comes even closer to the sun, the tails form. The gas tail is blown straight out by the solar wind, particles streaming out from the sun. The gas tail moves from side to side slightly and shows kinks as the solar wind changes. The dust is left behind, and is pushed back by the sunlight itself.

Halley's Comet came closest to the sun on February 9, 1986. Three weeks before this point in its orbit, known as its *perihelion*, a long tail had already formed. Unfortunately, when Halley's Comet was closest to the sun this time, it was on the opposite side of the sun from the Earth. So we couldn't get a good view.

A view of Halley's Comet, taken with a light-sensitive chip rather than film. The video image is displayed on a computer screen.

For the weeks around perihelion, Halley's Comet was too close to the sun for us to see. One spacecraft around Venus and one spacecraft in Earth orbit did observe it then.

Unfortunately, because of the relative positions of sun, Earth, and comet, the comet was not close to Earth when it was at its brightest. At almost all the previous passages, every 74 to 79 years since 240 B.C., Halley's Comet was brighter and showed a longer tail.

Comet tails always point away from the sun, no matter what direction a comet is traveling. Thus sometimes a comet's tail goes before the comet's head. One type of event that occurred more than a dozen times during this visit of Halley's Comet was the disconnection of its tail. As the solar wind (see p. 106) changes, the tail sometimes just drifts off behind the comet. As long as the comet is reasonably close to the sun, a new tail soon forms.

With all the advance notice of Halley's Comet, astronomers could reserve telescope time at the major observatories and could prepare special instruments and filters for observing the comet.

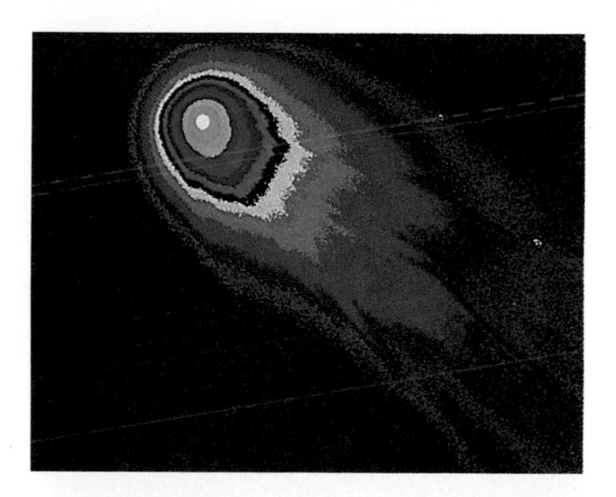

Instead of playing back the image of the comet as a photograph-like video picture, as on the opposite page, the computer can use the same information to color-code the comet's brightness, as shown here.

Halley's Comet (Close-up Views)

Because of the unprecedented advance notice of the comet's arrival, various nations could prepare spacecraft to go out to meet Halley's Comet. Close-up views showed us the nucleus of a comet for the first time. Halley's Comet has a nucleus that is potato-shaped, and is the size of a small town. It has small mountains and craters.

Halley's Comet is covered with a crust of dark material. Jets of dust spew out from cracks in the dark material.

The close-up views from the European Space Agency's spacecraft were the best. The spacecraft was named Giotto, after the 14th-century artist who used a drawing of Halley's Comet's 1301 visit as the Star of Bethlehem in a fresco.

Some of the jets viewed by the Giotto spacecraft masked the edge of the nucleus. Giotto flew by so fast that it got only a brief view. In fact, the spacecraft collided with a piece of dust just before it got closest to the comet's nucleus, and was set wobbling.

A view of Halley's Comet close up from the Giotto spacecraft. The field of view is only about 12 miles (20 km) across.

Halley's Comet from the Ground

The best broadside views of Halley's Comet came in the weeks after the spacecraft passed by. Astronomers at many observatories on Earth studied the comet through large optical and radio telescopes. Molecules like water and ammonia in the comet's coma and tail were observed. The Giotto spacecraft had measured that about 30 tons of water and 5 tons of dust were given off by the nucleus of the comet each hour.

Because of the angle at which Halley's Comet approached the Earth, the best views were from the Southern Hemisphere. Although many people traveled to Australia and other places in the Southern Hemisphere in hopes of obtaining a good view, the comet did not cooperate. In the middle of this prime time for tourist viewing, the comet's tail became disconnected and drifted off. Though the tail had drifted off several times before, this time the comet was too far from the sun for a new tail to form. Between this problem and the lack of good viewing from the Northern Hemisphere, most people on Earth never got a good view of Halley's Comet in 1986.

Halley's Comet against the Milky Way, viewed from Australia.

Halley's Comet

By May 1986, Halley's Comet had only a short, wide tail. Still, it was fun to see the comet as it moved from night to night against the background of stars.

As Halley's Comet travels outward in the solar system, it gets fainter. Its tail is gone. The Hubble Space Telescope should be able to observe it at any position in its orbit, so it may never disappear from view again.

Halley's Comet is due back near Earth in 2061. I hope some readers of this book will see it then. But 2061 won't be a favorable viewing either. The next good view people on Earth will have of Halley's Comet will be in May 2134. Perhaps by then anybody who wants to will be able to travel out to meet it.

All the studies of Halley's Comet gave us our most detailed view of this type of member of our solar system. The dirty-snowball theory (see p. 106) was upheld. However, because the mountain on the comet's nucleus remains, in spite of dozens of passages near the sun, the mountain may have some firm underpinning. Comets may, rather, be icy dirtballs.

Halley's Comet as it passed the globular star cluster known as Omega Centauri.

Sun-grazing Comets

A spacecraft that was in orbit for some time had the ability to create an artificial eclipse of the sun. The region near the sun was hidden, but the sun's upper corona could be seen. This spacecraft discovered over half a dozen comets that are "sun grazers." These comets come very close to the sun. The one shown in this picture was seen coming closer and closer to the sun but not receding. Instead, a "splash" appeared. Apparently, the comet hit the sun.

Why are we so interested in comets? Their beauty in the night sky and their usually unexpected appearance are part of the reason. But, comets also bring us material from very distant parts of the solar system. We think there is a cloud of chunks of ice and dust far beyond Pluto's orbit that contains comets. Every once in a while, gravity from a nearby star makes one of the comets fall in toward the sun. The gravity of Jupiter may make the comet go into a closed orbit. As the comet approaches the sun, it grows a tail.

The material from so far out in space has not changed in the 4 billion years since the solar system was formed. So by studying comets, we are studying the youth of the solar system.

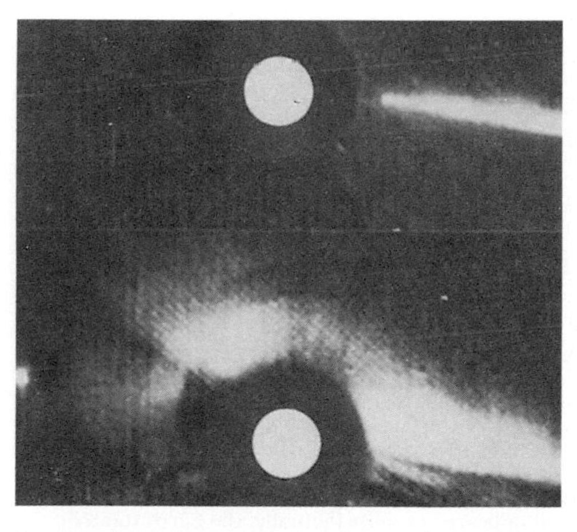

A series showing a sun-grazing comet, observed from a satellite that artificially hid the visible surface of the sun.

Meteors and Meteorites

Sometimes a bit of interplanetary space joins us on Earth. A meteor can flash through the sky, and we may even find a piece of it on Earth, as a meteorite.

Most of the meteors we see in the sky are comet dust. The dust spreads out in a comet's orbit, and at the same time every year, when the Earth goes through the comet's orbit, we see a meteor shower (see pp. 114–115). Each meteor looks like a "shooting star" in the sky. At the height of a big meteor shower, you may even see one meteor a minute.

Even at other times, we sometimes see meteors flashing across the sky. To see one, just go outside on a dark, clear night and look up. On the average, one meteor will go by every seven minutes.

Meteors can appear in any part of the sky. You can't know in advance where to look, so telescopes or binoculars are no help. Lying back on a blanket or a lawn chair placed far from trees or buildings is the best way to see meteors.

To photograph a meteor, set your camera on a tripod and take an exposure of several minutes. You may be lucky enough to capture a meteor on film.

A bright meteor flashes across the sky. The many trails are stars that appeared to move (actually, the Earth rotated) during the 4-minute tripod-based exposure. This meteor left a train that lasted a few seconds.

Fireballs

The brightest meteors are known as *fireballs.* They can be much brighter than any planet. A fireball is a glowing chunk of rock that may be a piece broken off an asteroid. Chunks of rock that we see as meteors are known as *meteoroids.* As the meteoroid passes through the Earth's atmosphere, friction heats it up so that it glows.

Sometimes, some of the rock survives the atmosphere's heating and lands on Earth. The part we find on Earth is called a *meteorite.*

Most of the meteorites we find when we see them fall are of a type called "stony" (see p. 114). They resemble ordinary stones, so we don't notice them otherwise. Most of the meteorites we find at other times are of a type called "irons" (see p. 115). They are made almost entirely of iron and nickel. They have a dark crust, from their fiery passage through our atmosphere. When irons are cut open and etched with acid, the exposed surfaces can take on beautiful patterns.

Many meteorites have been found in recent years in Antarctica. The snow preserves them and moving snow and ice concentrates them.

A fireball visible in the daytime sky is a rare occurrence.

Meteor Showers

If you are out during a meteor shower, you can try to sketch the paths of the meteors you see. If you trace the paths backward, you will find they all come from about the same point. That point is the *radiant*, or origin, of the shower. Each meteor shower is usually named after the constellation or star where it seems to originate: for example, the Orionids seem to come from the constellation Orion. (The Quadrantids have a name based on the name of a group of stars we no longer consider a constellation.)

Two of the meteor showers come from dust left by Halley's Comet. Both the Eta Aquarids in early May and the Orionids in late October are glowing bits of dust from Halley's Comet burning up in the Earth's atmosphere.

Before midnight on any night, you are on the part of Earth that is facing away from the direction Earth is traveling through space. But after midnight, you are on the side of Earth that is plowing into the meteor dust — the trail of a comet. So during a shower, you usually see more meteors after midnight.

The phase of the moon also affects how many meteors you see. Some years, a given shower occurs when the moon is full or nearly full. The sky is then too bright for many meteors to be seen.

The largest stony meteorite in a museum, the Ahnighito meteorite in the American Museum of Natural History in New York. It weighs 34 tons and was brought by William Peary and Matthew Henson from the Arctic.

The table below gives the dates when meteor showers are at or near their peak: that is, with a frequency at least one-fourth of their maximum rate. It also gives the average wait you may have between meteors when the shower is at its peak.

Two of the showers listed occur over a large number of nights, in November. But at any one time, you will probably not see the peak rate. You may also see other random meteors that are not part of a shower.

Some showers are better in some years than others. The Leonids are best about every 33 years. The Leonid shower should be exciting in 1998 and 1999.

Meteor Showers

Date	Name	Interval at Peak
January 3	Quadrantids	1 min.
April 21	Lyrids	4 min.
May 3–5	Eta Aquarids	3 min.
July 25–31	Delta Aquarids	3 min.
August 9–13	Perseids	1 min.
October 21	Orionids	2 min.
early November	South Taurids	4 min.
mid-November	Leonids	4 min.
December 12–14	Geminids	1 min.
December 22	Ursids	4 min.

An iron/nickel meteorite, the Goose Lake meteorite, in the Smithsonian Institution's National Museum of Natural History in Washington, D.C. It is the fourth largest iron ever discovered.

Asteroids

Starting in 1801, astronomers started to find additional planets. They soon realized that these were "minor planets," as opposed to the "major planets" like the Earth and Jupiter. We now know of over 4,000 minor planets, which are also known as asteroids. Asteroids have both names and numbers. The discoverers get to assign the names.

Astronomers think that the solar system formed as gas and dust collapsed by the force of its own gravity. The collapsing gas and dust formed a system shaped like a disk, because nothing could oppose gravity from top to bottom. Any small spin the gas and dust had before the collapse started made the disk spin faster as it grew smaller and more concentrated. (An ice skater, in the same way, spins faster with his or her arms pulled in.) The sun eventually formed at the middle of the collapsing disk. Small objects called planetesimals also formed.

Many planetesimals merged and were held together by their own gravity to form the major planets. Some planetesimals remain as asteroids or as moons.

The photographs on this page and on the facing page show a field of stars with an asteroid (just below the green rectangle) in it.

The first asteroid to be discovered was 1 Ceres. It is 635 miles (1,025 km) in diameter. The next largest is 2 Pallas. A few years ago, it passed in front of a star as seen from Earth. Many amateur astronomers spread out over a large region on Earth to time when the asteroid passed the star and made it wink out. By studying the results, scientists could deduce an accurate diameter and shape for 2 Pallas. It is 347 miles × 327 miles × 331 miles across (558 km × 526 km × 532 km). Many asteroids are too small to have enough gravity pulling toward their center to make them round.

As you might expect, the first asteroids to be discovered were among the largest and therefore the brightest. 3 Juno is 155 miles (249 km) across and 4 Vesta is 345 miles (555 km) across. Vesta comes close enough to Earth that it can barely be seen by the naked eye. A few dozen asteroids can be followed with binoculars.

As asteroids orbit the sun, they move with respect to the stars. They therefore stand out on photographs of the stars. If a telescope is tracking the stars (making them appear as points of light), then the asteroids appear as streaks.

Note the distance in the sky the asteroid has moved in the two-day interval between this photo and the one on the facing page.

Asteroids

All asteroids orbit the sun, as do all major planets. Most asteroids orbit in the "asteroid belt," located between the orbits of Mars and Jupiter. Sometimes they hit each other there, sending off chunks of rock to become fireballs and meteorites on Earth and on other planets.

Some asteroids orbit in different locations. The Apollo asteroids have orbits that cross the orbit of the Earth. The Aten asteroids not only cross the Earth's orbit but also have orbits with average diameter smaller than Earth's orbit. Some could hit our planet, with spectacular results. We know of a few dozen Aten and Apollo asteroids.

One of these asteroids probably hits the Earth every few hundred million years. A large asteroid hitting the Earth could throw up a lot of dust, hiding the sun. A theory is being studied that a collision of an asteroid with the Earth 65 million years ago led to the extinction of the dinosaurs and other species. One piece of evidence in favor of this theory is the fact that the element iridium, which is commonly found in asteroids, is widely distributed in a layer of Earth rock that we can date as being 65 million years old.

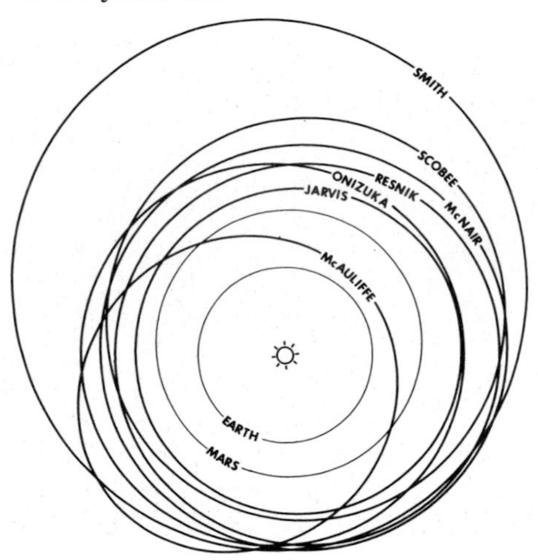

Seven of the asteroids, mostly in the asteroid belt, were named for the seven astronauts who died in the explosion of the Space Shuttle Challenger.

More than 200 asteroids are known to be larger than 65 miles (100 km) across. But all the asteroids together have less than 1/1000 the mass of the Earth. Nobody believes anymore the old idea that the asteroids are the remains of a planet that broke up.

We know a little about asteroids from studying three asteroids that we think were captured by planets' gravity. Phobos and Deimos — two moons orbiting around Mars — and Phoebe, which orbits around Saturn, may be captured asteroids. Phoebe, for example, orbits far beyond Saturn's other moons. It orbits in the plane of Saturn's orbit around the sun, rather than in the plane of the other moons around Saturn. It also orbits in the opposite direction from Saturn's other moons.

Asteroids come in several different types. Some are very dark. We can sometimes tell what kind of asteroid was the parent of a meteorite — an asteroid chip — we have on Earth.

We have plans for studying a couple of asteroids from space. The Galileo mission en route to Jupiter is intended to pass by an asteroid to make close-up measurements. Later, a special NASA mission called Comet Rendezvous — Asteroid Flyby (CRAF) is to fly by an asteroid while it is en route to a comet.

The green and blue trails are from the motion of an asteroid while photographs were taken one after the other through green and blue filters. The red photograph that also went into making this full-color print of a nebula (a cloud of gas and dust) was taken two weeks earlier, so the asteroid did not appear on it.

Other Solar Systems

Scientists, like most other people, want to know if there is life in the universe away from the Earth. Did life arise in several places by itself? Studies of Mars have not found signs of life there, though the presence of water shows that life could possibly have survived. The other planets and their moons seem less likely places for life as we know it.

We know that the sun has a solar system with nine major planets, as well as comets, asteroids, and meteoroids. Do other stars have solar systems? Are there other planets? In spite of trying very hard, no astronomer has ever seen a planet around another star. But there are some reports that the gravity of some large planets may be changing the motion of some nearby stars. Studies continue.

Some of the best evidence for other solar systems is the observation on this page of the southern star named beta Pictoris. Astronomers placed a small disk into their telescope to block out the light from the star itself. Then the fainter light from around the star could be seen. The false-color image below shows a disk that could resemble the disk of gas and dust from which our solar system formed. We could be seeing a solar system in formation.

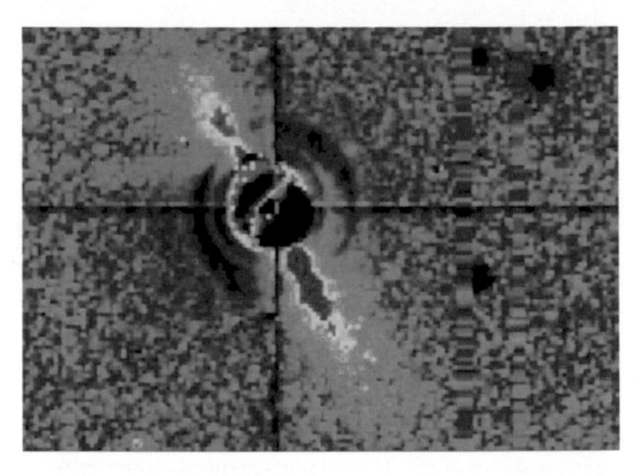

In this false-color view, the star beta Pictoris has been blocked, allowing astronomers to photograph a disk of gas and dust surrounding it.

The Search for Life in the Universe

Astronomers are trying hard to find objects in the universe that are smaller than stars. An object is a star when nuclear fusion takes place inside it (see p. 97). Objects with slightly too little mass to become a star are "brown dwarfs." They would be too faint to see in ordinary light but might show in infrared light. Reports have been made that brown dwarfs have been discovered.

Even if another solar system were found, that would be a far cry from detecting life within it. Some astronomers are even using radio telescopes to tell if intelligent beings somewhere far away are trying to send us signals. Searches have been going on for decades. The quality of the searches continues to improve as advances in electronics allow us to make better samples. We have many directions to look in and many frequencies to try.

Hoping to find signals from life in the universe is very different from believing that visitors from outer space are here. Most astronomers are sorry that so many people believe in UFO's, or "unidentified flying objects." Whenever we have enough information, the UFO's can be explained as normal phenomena in the Earth's atmosphere or in the sky.

An artist's idea of a set of radio telescopes designed to be placed in craters on the far side of the moon. Protected from the Earth's radio signals by the bulk of the moon, they would be able to make sensitive searches for signals from beings far away.

Facts About Our Solar System

Object	Radius of Object (in km)	Radius of Orbit (in km)	Radius of Orbit (÷ Earth's)	Period of Orbit
MERCURY	2,439	58,000,000	0.4	0.24 year
no moon				
VENUS	6,052	108,000,000	0.7	0.62 year
no moon				
EARTH	6,378	150,000,000	1.0	1.00 year
The Moon	1,738	384,500		27 days
MARS	3,393	228,000,000	1.5	1.88 year
Phobos	14×10×9	9,378		8 hours
Deimos	8×6×5	23,459		30 hours
JUPITER	71,400	778,000,000	5.2	11.9 years
Adrastea	12×10×8	127,000		7 hours
Metis	20	129,000		7 hours
Amalthea	130×85×80	180,000		12 hours
Thebe	55×45	222,000		16 hours
Io	1,815	422,000		42 hours
Europa	1,569	671,000		85 hours
Ganymede	2,631	1,070,000		7 days
Callisto	2,400	1,883,000		17 days
Leda	10	11,094,000		240 days
Himalia	90	11,480,000		251 days
Lysithea	20	11,720,000		260 days
Elara	40	11,740,000		260 days
Ananke	15	21,200,000		617 days
Carme	20	22,600,000		692 days
Pasiphae	20	23,500,000		735 days
Sinope	20	23,700,000		758 days
SATURN	60,000	1,427,000	9.5	29.5 years
Atlas	20×10	137,670		14 hours
Prome-theus	70×50×40	139,353		15 hours
Pandora	55×45×35	141,700		15 hours
Janus	110×100×80	151,400		17 hours
Epime-theus	70×60×50	151,400		17 hours
Mimas	195	185,500		23 hours
Enceladus	255	238,000		33 hours
Tethys	525	294,700		42 hours
Telesto	17×14×13	294,700		42 hours
Calypso	17×11×11	294,700		42 hours
Dione	560	377,400		66 hours
Helene	18×16×15	378,060		66 hours
Rhea	765	527,000		108 hours
Titan	2575	1,221,800		16 days
Hyperion	205×125×110	1,481,100		21 days
Iapetus	730	3,561,300		79 days
Phoebe	110	12,952,000		549 days

Object	Radius of Object (in km)	Radius of Orbit (in km)	Radius of Orbit (÷ Earth's)	Period of Orbit
URANUS	26,071	2,871,000	19.2	84.1 years
Cordelia	20	49,771		8 hours
Ophelia	25	53,796		9 hours
Bianca	25	59,173		10 hours
Cressida	30	61,777		11 hours
Desdemona	30	62,676		11 hours
Juliet	40	64,352		12 hours
Portia	40	66,085		12 hours
Rosalind	30	69,942		12 hours
Belinda	30	75,258		15 hours
Puck	85	86,000		18 hours
Miranda	242	129,783		34 hours
Ariel	580	191,239		60 hours
Umbriel	595	265,969		99 hours
Titania	805	435,844		209 hours
Oberon	775	582,596		323 hours
NEPTUNE	24,300	4,497,000	30.1	164 years
inner ring		42,000		
1989N6	25	48,200		7 hours
1989N5	45	50,100		7.5 hours
1989N3	70	52,500		8 hours
1989N4	80	62,000		10 hours
outer ring		63,000		
1989N2	100	73,500		13 hours
1989N1	210	117,600		27 hours
Triton	1,360	354,800		6 days
Nereid	170	5,513,400		360 days
PLUTO	1,142	5,913,000	39.5	249 years
Charon	600	19,000		153 hours

Conversions

1 A.U. (astronomical unit*) = 1,495,978.70 km = 92,958,348 miles

1 year (Earth year) = 365.242 198 78 days = 31,558,150 seconds

mass of sun = 1.981×10^{30} kg

mass of Earth = 5.9742×10^{24} kg

mass of our moon = 7.35×10^{22} kg

(mass of sun):(mass of Earth) = 333,000:1

(mass of Earth):(mass of our moon) = 81.3:1

***Note:** One astronomical unit (1 A.U.) is equivalent to the average distance between the Earth and the sun.

Credits

Front cover NASA/Jet Propulsion Laboratory
4–5, 6–7 © 1986 Hanşen Planetarium, Salt Lake City, Utah; reproduced with permission
8, 9, 12, 13, 27–29, 41 NASA/Johnson Space Center
10 O. Brown, R. Evans, and M. Carle, University of Miami Rosenstiel School of Marine and Atmospheric Science
11 Gene Carl Feldman, Compton J. Tucker—NASA/Goddard Space Flight Center
14–15 NASA
16 R. E. Wallace, U.S. Geological Survey
17–18, 34–35, 42–43, 57, 99–100, 114–115 Jay M. Pasachoff
19–25, 103 Williams College—Hopkins Observatory/Kevin Reardon
26, 109 Akira Fujii
30, 116—117 Dennis Milon
31–32, 45–46, 48–50, 58–64, 69–77, 80–91 NASA/Jet Propulsion Laboratory
33 U.S. Geological Survey
36 William M. Sinton and Klaus Hodapp (Institute for Astronomy, University of Hawaii), David Crisp (Caltech), B. Ragent (NASA/Ames Research Center), and D. Allen (Anglo-Australian Observatory)
37, 40, 121 NASA/Ames Research Center
38 Academy of Sciences, U.S.S.R., and James Head, Brown University
39 NASA/Gordon Pettingill, MIT/U.S. Geological Survey
44 Lowell Observatory photograph by L. J. Martin at Mauna Kea Observatory; processing by U.S. Geological Survey, Branch of Astrogeology; observations supported by the National Geographic Society
47 Alfred McEwen, U.S. Geological Survey
51 Space Research Institute, Academy of Sciences, U.S.S.R., courtesy G. Avanesov
52–55, 66–67, 78–79 Wil Tirion
56 Alberto Ossola
65 Mark R. Showalter, NASA/Ames Research Center
68 Lunar and Planetary Laboratory, University of Arizona
92 Carol A. Christian and Patrick Waddell, Canada-France-Hawaii Telescope Corporation
93 Mark V. Sykes, Steward Observatory, University of Arizona
94 G. Baier and G. Weigelt, Physikalisches Institut, Universität Erlangen-Nürnberg
95 John R. Spencer, Institute for Astronomy, University of Hawaii
96 Williams College—Hopkins Observatory/Arielle Kagan and Jay M. Pasachoff
97 K. Libbrecht, Big Bear Solar Observatory, Caltech, with calculations by J. Christensen-Dalsgaard, J. Schou, P. Goode, and W. Dziembowski
98 Norikura Solar Observatory, courtesy of E. Hiei
101 Harvard-Smithsonian Center for Astrophysics
102 R. J. Poole/DayStar Filter Corp.
104 Serge Koutchmy

105 Jay M. Pasachoff, Dale P. Cruikshank, Clark R. Chapman

106–107 Uwe Fink, Alfred B. Schultz, Michael A. DiSanti, and Reiner Fink, University of Arizona

108 © 1986 Max-Planck Institut für Aeronomie, Lindau/Hartz, FRG; photographed with the Halley Multicolour Camera aboard the European Space Agency's Giotto spacecraft, courtesy H. U. Keller

110 © 1986 William Liller. All rights reserved.

111 Neil R. Sheeley, Jr., Naval Research Laboratory

112 Michael Shin

113 © James M. Baker

118 Edward Bowell, Lowell Observatory

119 © 1979 Royal Observatory Edinburgh/Anglo-Australian Telescope Board, photograph by David Malin from original U.K. Schmidt plates

120 R. J. Terrile, NASA/Jet Propulsion Laboratory, and B. A. Smith, University of Arizona, with Carnegie Institution of Washington's Las Campanas Observatory, Chile

Index

Page numbers in **bold** indicate main discussion. Page numbers in *italics* indicate illustrations.

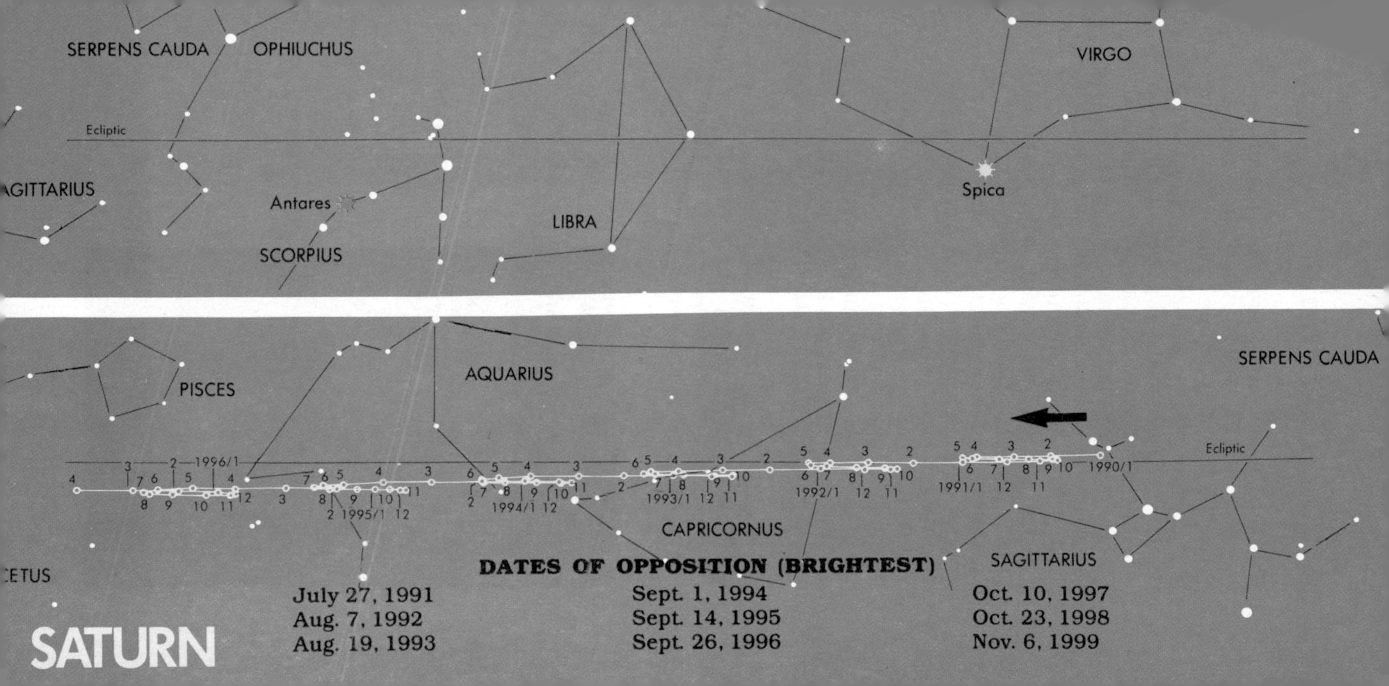
SERPENS CAUDA
OPHIUCHUS
VIRGO
Ecliptic
AGITTARIUS
Antares
SCORPIUS
LIBRA
Spica
PISCES
AQUARIUS
SERPENS CAUDA
Ecliptic
1996/1
1995/1
1994/1
1993/1
1992/1
1991/1
1990/1
CAPRICORNUS
SAGITTARIUS
CETUS
DATES OF OPPOSITION (BRIGHTEST)
July 27, 1991
Aug. 7, 1992
Aug. 19, 1993
Sept. 1, 1994
Sept. 14, 1995
Sept. 26, 1996
Oct. 10, 1997
Oct. 23, 1998
Nov. 6, 1999
SATURN

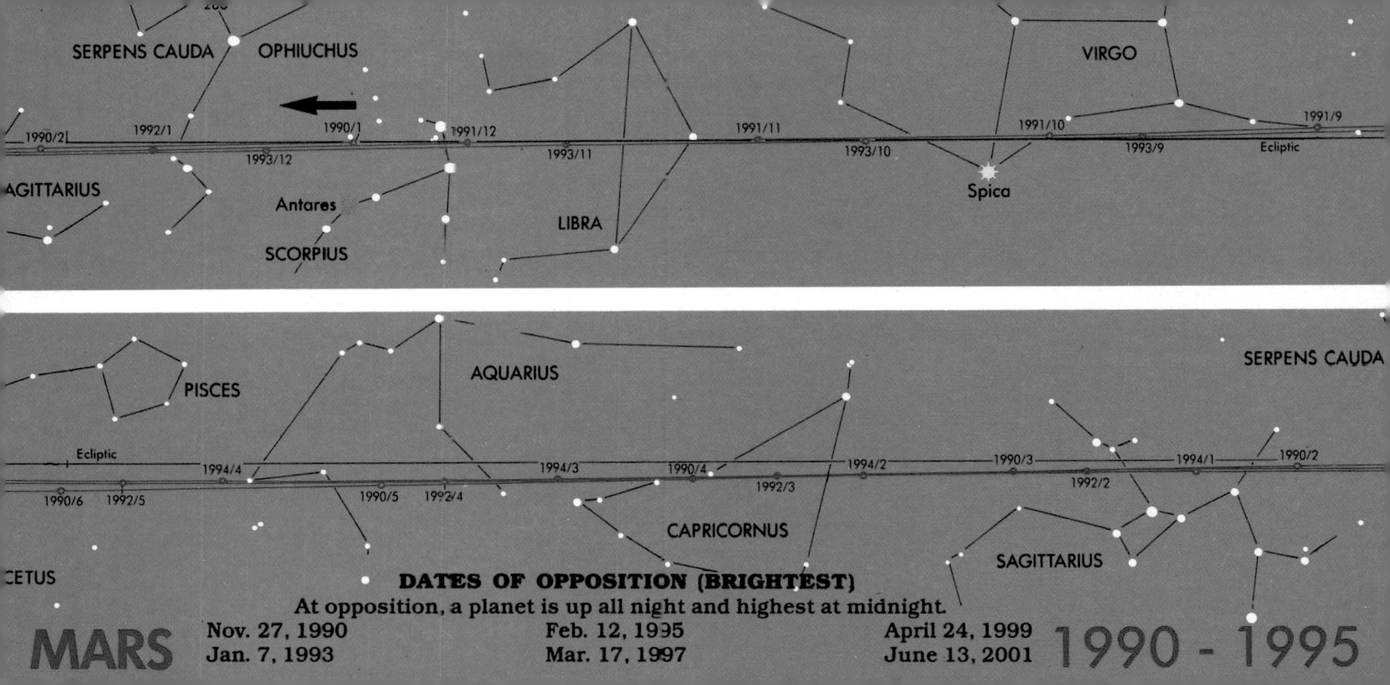
SERPENS CAUDA
OPHIUCHUS
VIRGO
1990/2
1992/1
1990/1
1991/12
1991/11
1991/10
1991/9
1993/12
1993/11
1993/10
1993/9
Ecliptic
SAGITTARIUS
Antares
SCORPIUS
LIBRA
Spica
PISCES
AQUARIUS
SERPENS CAUDA
Ecliptic
1994/4
1994/3
1990/4
1994/2
1990/3
1994/1
1990/2
1990/6
1992/5
1990/5
1992/4
1992/3
1992/2
CAPRICORNUS
SAGITTARIUS
CETUS
DATES OF OPPOSITION (BRIGHTEST)
At opposition, a planet is up all night and highest at midnight.
Nov. 27, 1990
Jan. 7, 1993
Feb. 12, 1995
Mar. 17, 1997
April 24, 1999
June 13, 2001
MARS 1990 - 1995

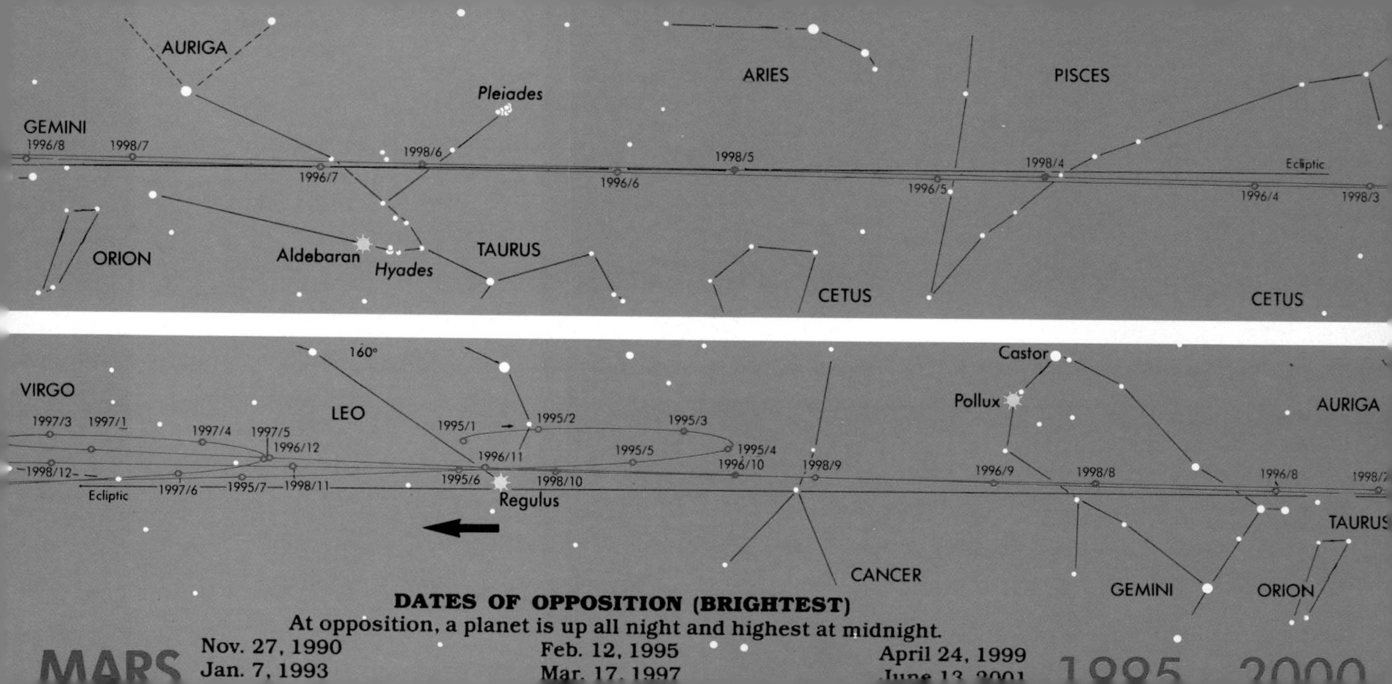

DATES OF OPPOSITION (BRIGHTEST)

At opposition, a planet is up all night and highest at midnight.

Nov. 27, 1990	Feb. 12, 1995	April 24, 1999
Jan. 7, 1993	Mar. 17, 1997	June 13, 2001